I MISS
            YOU
WHEN I
        BLINK

**Also by Mary Laura Philpott**

*Penguins with People Problems*

# I MISS YOU WHEN I BLINK

*Essays*

## MARY LAURA PHILPOTT

**ATRIA** BOOKS

New York   London   Toronto   Sydney   New Delhi

ATRIA
BOOKS

An Imprint of Simon & Schuster, Inc.
1230 Avenue of the Americas
New York, NY 10020

First Atria Books hardcover edition April 2019

**ATRIA** B O O K S and colophon are registered trademarks
of Simon & Schuster, Inc.

For information about special discounts for bulk purchases,
please contact Simon & Schuster Special Sales at 1-866-506-1949
or business@simonandschuster.com.

The Simon & Schuster Speakers Bureau can bring authors to
your live event. For more information or to book an event,
contact the Simon & Schuster Speakers Bureau at 866-248-3049
or visit our website at www.simonspeakers.com.

Interior design by Kyle Kabel

Manufactured in the United States of America

10  9  8  7  6  5  4  3  2  1

Library of Congress Cataloging-in-Publication Data
Names: Philpott, Mary Laura, author.
Title: I miss you when I blink : essays / Mary Laura Philpott.
Description: New York : Atria, [2019] |
Identifiers: LCCN 2018030497 (print) | LCCN 2018050689 (ebook) | ISBN
   9781982102821 (eBook) | ISBN 9781982102807 (hardcover) | ISBN
   9781982102814 (pbk.) | ISBN 9781982102821 (ebk.)
Subjects: LCSH: Philpott, Mary Laura. | Middle-aged women--United
   States--Biography. | Women authors, American--Biography. | Television talk
   show hosts--United States--Biography. | Women--Humor. | Adulthood--Humor.
Classification: LCC CT275. P5937 (ebook) | LCC CT275. P5937 A3 2019 (print) |
   DDC 305.244/2092--dc23
LC record available at https://lccn.loc.gov/2018030497

ISBN 978-1-9821-0280-7
ISBN 978-1-9821-0282-1 (ebook)

*For John*
*For my parents*
*For WC and MG*

We know, we know, we belong to ya
We know you threw your arms around us
In the hopes we wouldn't change
But we had to change some
You know, to belong to you

—The Decemberists,
    "The Singer Addresses His Audience"

# Contents

# CONTENTS

# I Miss You When I Blink

**It's** the perfect sentence, but I didn't write it. My six-year-old did.

I was sitting at the desk in my home office, on a copywriting deadline for a client in the luggage industry, wrestling with a paragraph about suitcases. I leaned forward, as if putting my face closer to the computer could help the words on the screen make garment bags sound exciting. My little boy lay on his belly on the rug, "working" to pass the time until our promised walk to the park. He murmured to himself as he scribbled with a yellow pencil stub on one of my notepads.

". . . and I miss you when I blink . . ." he said.

It stopped me mid-thought. "Say that again?"

"I miss you when I blink," he answered, and looked up, pleased to have caught my attention. He turned back to his notepad, chattering on with his rhyme (*I miss you in the sink . . . I miss you in a skating rink . . .*). When he ripped off the page and tossed it aside, I picked it up and pinned it to the bulletin board on my office wall.

I turned those words over in my mind while I folded laundry that afternoon. I thought about them while I brushed my teeth that evening. I repeated them to myself as I lay awake in bed. I said them out loud as I sat in traffic the next day. *I miss you when I blink*. I thought, *How cute*.

Over the next several months, I saw the note on the wall every time I walked into my office, and the phrase lodged itself in my head like a song lyric. I played with the words when I had writer's block, tossing them about like a squishy stress ball. It would make a great title for a sappy love poem, I thought, one where the poet can't stand to lose sight of his lover even for a split second. Or an album of goodbye songs, dedicated to a time or place that's disappeared. Maybe a country ballad about a lost hound dog. The one that got away. Anyone could be the "you."

It was a few years later when it occurred to me: You could even say it to yourself.

We all keep certain phrases handy in our minds—hanging on hooks just inside the door where we can grab them like a raincoat, for easy access. Not mantras exactly, but go-to choruses that state how things are, that give structure to the chaos and help life make a little more sense.

A friend of mine uses "not my circus, not my monkeys" a lot. It helps her ignore her instinct to get involved in things that aren't her business, and it also makes her remember that people have all sorts of reasons for the things they do, many of which she'll never understand. It's useful for both behavior modification and acceptance.

"No one's getting out of here alive" is one of mine. I find it motivational and comforting. I say it to myself when I'm marching along on the elliptical machine, because it reminds me that there absolutely will come an end to my time on earth, and if I want to push it off as far into the distance as I can, I need to get my heart strong and work off the sugar I consume every day. I say it to myself when I'm trying to calm down and deal with a jerk, because it helps me put things in perspective. We're all going to die, and would I really die with more points if I took this person down, or should I have some empathy and grace and let our differences go?

Over time, "I miss you when I blink" became another one of these phrases. It helps me live in the moment. It slows me down and makes me absorb each instant instead of rushing, because I know already how much I miss things that happened in the past—how they're right there behind my eyelids but also gone forever. When my now-teenage son is doing something very teenage son and I'm having to ask him for the eighth time in one evening to pick up his inside-out pants from the bathroom floor, "I miss you when I blink" helps me be more patient. He was six just a second ago. He'll grow up and leave me in another second. "I miss you when I blink." It captures the depths of my love. Could he have meant all this when he was little and scribbling, or was he just trying to rhyme with "sink"?

There's no way he could have known.

So he also couldn't have realized how perfectly "I miss you when I blink" captures that universal adult experience: the identity crisis. But there it is.

The old stereotypical identity crisis happens in midlife, to a man, and it features a twenty-five-year-old dental hygienist and a pricey sports car with an engine that sounds like a helicopter. The new stereotypical identity crisis happens to a woman, often when she's turning forty, and it involves either a lengthy stay in Tuscany (ideally in a picturesque cottage) or a very long hike (maybe the trail to Machu Picchu? preferably with a large backpack). But the "I miss you when I blink" kind of identity crisis, that's something else. Something under the radar, much more common.

For so many people I know, there is no one big midlife smashup; there's a recurring sense of having met an impasse, a need to turn around and not only change course, but change *the way you are*. It can happen anytime and many times. As we leave school and enter the real world, as we move in and out of friendships and romances, as we reckon with professional choices and future plans, and sure, when we hit midlife, but earlier and later, too.

I think this repeated need for recalibration happens partly because so many ways of being are pitched to us—particularly to women—as either-or choices: You can have a career or a family; be a domestic goddess who cans her own strawberry jam or a train wreck who flaunts the wine in her coffee mug; wear a blazer and tote a bullet journal or stick pencils in your messy bun and wipe paint on your jeans. Pious or profane. One thing or the other. Even whether or not you buy into those dichotomies seems to be an either-or proposition: You believe in "having it all" or you believe "having it all" is out-dated bunk. Pick a way.

And it's true that at any given second, a person is doing one thing or another. I can swallow a bite of toast right now *or* I can whistle the theme song from *House of Cards*. I can't do both at the exact same moment or I'll choke. But our lives aren't one suspended moment, a single either-or choice; they're a string of moments, a string of choices. Going from one moment to the next is not always a comfortable process. Sometimes it hurts, like when you realize your child no longer needs you to be his daily sidekick, and you have to adjust to a new role in his life. Sometimes it's a comedy of errors, like when you decide you're ready for a fresh start and you buy a whole wardrobe of pants and blouses that seem sleek and smart in the dressing room but in the light of day make you look like you're about to give a PowerPoint presentation on a golf course. Sometimes you know one phase of life is ending—you've outgrown a relationship or reached the end of a long project—but you don't know what the next step is supposed to be. You feel sure you can't go forward and you can't go back and you absolutely, positively cannot stand still one minute longer, all of which is insanely frustrating.

That's what small identity shifts look like in everyday lives. Not the stereotypes.

The kind of crucial points in life I'm talking about are the ones that often go unseen, that most of us would feel embarrassed to call crises. They're the ones a friend might talk about while sitting on your front steps in the dark at midnight after a dinner party, stalling because she doesn't want to go home. Or because she hates her job. Or she's scared something's wrong with her kid or her spouse. Or she just saw one of her notebooks from college in a drawer, and she feels so detached from the person who wrote those brilliant notes about Virginia Woolf, and she's worried that smart twenty-year-old has disappeared and she'll never get her back, but she thinks she might want to try. She misses herself when she blinks.

*I miss you when I blink*. I have felt it so many times in my life, at points where I didn't really know who I was anymore, where I felt that when I closed my eyes, I could feel myself gone.

I still have that scrap of paper my son wrote on all those years ago, before I had any clue that what he was writing would become my touchstone. I didn't know then what a versatile refrain it would become.

I use it all the time. When I feel pressure to do the one exactly right thing—which I feel all the time because I am a human and a perfectionist—I remember all the selves I simultaneously have been, am, and will be. *I miss you when I blink* means *I know all my selves are here with me, and I know we can do this.* Saying it to myself is like a coach pushing a player out onto the field and saying, "You've got it. Just do what we practiced." It's like a parent placing a hand on the shoulder of an almost-grown child heading out the door to the prom, saying, "Remember who you are."

Sometimes I think, *Dammit, I will never be fifteen or twenty-five or thirty-five again. Those lives I've lived are over.* And I get a little wistful, thinking I might like to get some of that time back. But then I remember my twenty-one-year-old self sitting in my cubicle at my first job out of college, feeling utterly confused and wishing she could disappear, and I think, *Hey, young-me, it gets better. I swear. Worse sometimes, but also better.*

And when I have anxiety attacks about the future—*What if right now is the happiest I will ever be and I'm not appreciating it enough? Will I reach the end of my days having never lived in France or made enough people happy or learned everything there is to know about outer space or being able to do a split? Am I eating enough anti-oxidants? What will I be doing in ten years? In twenty?*—I say *I miss you when I blink* to myself, and it means, *Get a grip. Don't panic. To figure out where to go next, look at where you came from. If you got here, you can get to the next thing.*

Sometimes, in moments of memory or daydream, I feel the different iterations of myself pass by each other, as if right-now-me crosses paths with past-me or imaginary-me or even future-me in the hallways of my mind. "I miss you when I blink," one says. "I'm right here," says the other, and reaches out a hand.

# Everything to
# Be Happy About

I was born without a sense of direction.

All babies are, I guess. But like wisdom teeth that never break through, my internal compass just didn't come in.

Once, after a delayed flight home from one of my first business trips, I trudged out of the Atlanta airport terminal at 2 a.m. and couldn't find my car in the parking lot. It wasn't where I left it, I was sure. Had it been stolen? I wandered around under flickering yellow lights, dragging my bags along the asphalt, breaking down into self-pitying sobs as if I'd been left behind on Mars by my fellow astronauts.

I walked up the up ramp, then found myself at a dead end at the top of the lot. So I turned around and followed the down ramps until I ended up in the basement, standing in front of a blank concrete slab. What kind of Hotel fucking California was this? In a panic, I retraced my steps and went back to where I'd started. The backs of my heels chafed and burned under the leather of my black pumps, so appropriate for sitting in a conference room and so ill-suited for half an hour of airport laps. I'd covered the whole lot twice and not passed my car. I would never get home. I was stuck.

I called and woke up John, my husband of just two months, and begged him to come get me.

"You're fine," he reassured me. "By the time I could get there, you'll find it."

I didn't find it. I found, instead, the airport security trailer. I knocked on the door, hoping this scene wouldn't become the beginning of the investigative journalism piece about my grisly death. A gray-haired guard wearing a navy uniform greeted me with a set of keys in his hand. He took his time walking to a truck with orange lights on top—tired and unimpressed by my lostness, as if he did this a few times every night—and I followed him, climbing into the front seat of a truck cab that smelled like corn chips and motor oil. We rode together from level to level, lot to lot, I with my face turned to the hot parking-lot air and my arm out the window, clicking the button on my automatic key.

After about ten minutes I heard a *beep-beep* and saw a flash of headlights. There was my car, waiting in a spot that didn't look familiar at all. I had to have passed it earlier. How had I missed it?

When I got home, John asked, "What happened?"

"I got trapped," I said. "But I escaped."

As turned around as I got in that parking lot, I get twice as confused driving on actual roads. I hate it when people give directions like, "Drive south for two miles," or, "Go east on the highway." How the hell do people know which way south and east are?

I need landmarks. If I have to get from point A to point D, I need to know what points B and C look like. Turn left at the red light just before the giant pothole. Veer right at the big billboard with a chicken on it. Stop when you get to the building with the bright blue roof. That's why now, whenever I'm in an unfamiliar parking lot, I take a photo of my spot and keep taking photos the whole way into the building so I can find my way back along the breadcrumbs I leave for myself: There's the Coke machine; there's the green EXIT sign; there's the revolving door. I drive with a robotic voice narrating my turns, my destination always plugged into a map app, even at home in my own city. I really can't overstate how much the iPhone has changed my life.

Fifteen years after that parking lot episode, I got lost again.

I didn't want to tell anyone I was unhappy, because it didn't make sense.

There was plenty of love and time to go around for our family, enough money for groceries and gas and the mortgage and even unexpected things like exploding water heaters and tree limbs through the roof. I had my health, my youth. I was not yet forty. I was not dying of an insidious cancer, and I had not accidentally gotten hooked on meth, like those soccer moms I saw on the news. My husband and children and parents were all alive and well.

And plenty was going right. Truly, if I picked different snapshots from this time in my life, they'd add up to a picture of perfection. I was still, sometimes, having fun. I did things with my family and friends. I worked. I posted cute pictures of my dogs online. Those are the moments people could see.

But then there were moments most people didn't see. Ask anyone who has lived through depression, and chances are at least some of them will tell you it was the most unlikely thing—that they had everything to be happy about. But even the people who have no terrible, obvious burden to carry can find themselves staggering under the weight of a dull, constant dread. It doesn't add up, but it's true.

Everything around me was as I'd designed it: There was the house we bought because it had the right number of bedrooms and a backyard flat enough for a swing set. There were the booster seats I meticulously researched and purchased—for our own children to ride in, plus the neighbor kids we carpooled with every day. I drove them to the elementary school we chose for its small classes and robust arts program and active parent association, for which I could volunteer on committees where the other parents might just be so inspired by my helpfulness that they'd write me thank-you notes in honor of my commitment and reliability. The house and the car seats and the school were part of the life we decided to live in the middle of Atlanta, the part of the city with the highest traffic, highest taxes, and highest crime, but also the highest density of culture and friends and activity. John and I agreed: We'd rather stab ourselves in the eyes than live in the suburbs. We were glad to pay more for less space in the name of authenticity. Screw the strip malls.

There was the basement I turned into an office, where I

did my job as a freelance writer and cartoonist. This twelve-by-fifteen-foot space had a little desk and a discarded dining-turned-writing chair and a tiny patch of rug thrown over the concrete floor to make it feel warmer and less like an underground bunker. The walls were exposed brick, and over the desk, light shone through a single window. No one else was using the room. I had laid claim to it because I felt the lack of a place that was mine, where no one could drop their socks or trash or half-empty cups, where I could leave out a stack of paper and not come back in an hour to find a crayon line drawn across every page. To make people laugh, I called it my "lady cave," which, instead of sounding cool, like "man cave," sounded like a coy euphemism for "vagina." But it was an ideal space for writing and drawing, occupations I chose because they allowed me to do what I love—fit ideas into word puzzles, doodle animals, and help people communicate more clearly. I had a schedule that was under my own control. All of this was under my own control, in fact, because I decided it all.

So why did I feel like I couldn't wake up from a classic anxiety dream in which I was stuck in traffic, watching the minutes tick by on a clock, knowing with certain dread that I was late, but not remembering where I was supposed to be going or how to get there?


I made all the turns that led me to where I ended up, feeling broken and low despite all the luck and support that should have made me feel safe and happy and secure.

Most of those decisions were right in the moment when I

made them. Well, some were terribly wrong. (See: the enormous SUV I purchased after my second child was born, then drove for a decade despite the fact that I couldn't park it and regularly crashed it into obstacles and other cars.) But mostly I made what I really believed were good choices. Even if you deliberately choose to do a "wrong" thing, you're choosing it, which means you've picked it as the right thing to do.

Still. You can stand by your past decisions even if they took you to a present where you don't belong anymore.

You can find yourself at a time when, no matter how many things you've done right—really, truly *right* in the moment when you did them—you feel like something is wrong. No, *everything* is wrong. This feeling will defy logic, which will make you nuts because you love logic! You believe in cause and effect, hard work that pays off, wise choices that reap rewards. Early to bed, early to rise, rinse with cold water, choose brown rice, save your money, wear sunscreen, don't lick water fountains, floss. These are not just things you believe; they're things you *do* because that's the deal: Do what's right, and you'll be glad in the end! If X, then Y.

But you're not glad. X, but not Y. The to-do list was supposed to get smaller and smaller as you checked off everything you meant to do and approached the finish line of bona fide adulthood. Instead, you got to the end of the list and didn't feel like you'd arrived anywhere. You felt more disoriented than ever.

I did, anyway.


I knew what to do when I felt lost: Find help. So I started seeing a therapist.

One morning, she leaned forward from her chair to where I sat cross-legged on a sofa and asked, "Can you pinpoint when you *stopped* feeling happy?"

"I . . ." I looked down at my lap.

I felt embarrassed because here I was in a psychiatric session that cost real money, using up daylight hours, trying to find out if my brain was defective, parsing my own happiness history as if it was something that mattered in the world. I was a cliché: first-world problems. I felt ashamed.

But she had a point. Maybe if I could figure out what situations made me feel *not like this*, I could find a path out of this state, and I could find it before my misery caused anyone else unhappiness. I started thinking, *I don't belong here anymore. I have to get out. Now.*

To find the path, I studied what other people did. I read books for guidance. How do other people get happy again? *Run away* was a common narrative. *Leave it all behind.* I read memoir after memoir by people who burned down one life and started another. *Scorch the earth and be reborn as someone new.* I could use that map if I wanted to. Maybe I should disappear into a crowded street on the other side of the world! Maybe I should change my name and climb a mountain! I researched tents. I put my hair in two braids and wrapped a bandana around my forehead: Does this look outdoorsy? And then I remembered, wait—I can't lift my carry-on bag into the overhead bin on a plane, much less haul a pack on my back all day. I'm not that person. Nor am I the other people whose life stories I devoured: the young woman who escaped a kidnapper's underground lair, the man who left a cult, or any of the many bold and exceptional individuals who chronicled their change of name, change of gender, change of everything in the search for who they really are.

I'm just a person.

It wouldn't be fair for me to say, "I'm just an average person," or "an ordinary" person, because I am also a lucky person. I was raised in a loving home and grew up to have another loving home, and I do not suffer from the dire physical, financial, or situational disadvantages that so many people struggle under.

But being fortunate doesn't mean you won't reach a certain point in life—many points, actually—and panic. It doesn't mean you don't periodically wonder how you got where you are and if there's any way to get out.

I tried to imagine myself an action-movie hero, tossing a match over my shoulder and walking off in slow motion as an explosion bloomed behind me. The problem is that if you toss a match like that, you can't control what it burns, and there was so much in my life I *didn't* want to burn down.

Surely, that wasn't the only alternative to the status quo. It couldn't be just this one-or-the-other choice. But if these weren't my only two options—stay miserable or blow it all up—then . . . what?

I was going to have to draw my own damned map.

# The Perfect Murder Weapon

I have lost so much sleep trying to figure out where to hide bodies.

Killers on television are always tossing their victims into shallow woodland graves or dumping them into rivers where hikers and fishermen will come across them the next day. If the perps are a little smarter, they try to cover their tracks by throwing acid all over everything or setting a fire. But they always leave something behind—a hair, a clothing fiber, a footprint. If you want to make someone disappear, you've got to think things through. Murder is no occasion for shoddy preparation. It's not like packing for a trip and then realizing, *Whoops! Forgot my underwear!* If you *Whoops! Forgot my glove!* back at the scene, you're toast.

Bad guys on TV also like to choose weapons that can be traced: a bullet from a specific gun, a knife with a telltale blade pattern, poison that leaves a chemical residue. Are they *trying* to get arrested? Do they not even want to do a good job? You'd think this would be a situation where somebody would take the time to check their work.

———

This line of thinking is why I've decided to quit watching crime shows and police procedurals before bedtime.

Every time I do, I stay awake for hours walking through the crime, planning how I'd have done it better, what weapon I'd have chosen. Not because I have plans to kill anyone—no, no, I'm the kind of person who rescues earthworms from sidewalks when the sun comes out after a rainstorm—but because I can't see a problem without trying to solve it. Even problems I don't have, problems that couldn't possibly have less to do with me, like how to pull off a well-organized, shipshape, evidence-free murder.

My name is Mary Laura, and I am addicted to getting things right.

All of us have some prevalent personality trait, no matter what other qualities we possess. There's always one ingredient that flavors everything else about us. The cilantro, if you will.

For me, it's my type A nature. I became aware of this label as a preteen, when a sixth-grade science teacher walked past my tidy desk and remarked offhandedly, "You're a little type A, aren't you?" I took note of her comment, keen to think she meant I was an A student. Over time, as I heard it more and more, I came to realize that being "type A" doesn't mean you're a grade A human being—it means you have a certain set of high-strung tendencies.

Back in the 1950s, a couple of cardiologists named Meyer Friedman and Ray Rosenman coined the term to describe people who were extraordinarily driven by work, more ambitious, competitive, and time-focused than most other people. They theorized that type A people, unlike their more naturally relaxed type B counterparts, had a higher risk of heart disease. (As it turned out, they were partially right. Research eventually proved a link between heart attacks and high levels of unreleased stress, and as all of us type A people can tell you, unreleased stress is what we have pulsing through our veins.) Nowadays the term is thrown around casually to mean anyone who's a stickler for timeliness, someone who fixates on perfection. In search of that perfection, some type A folks see other people as competitors in everything they do. Others (like me) compete constantly with themselves, always trying to beat their own personal best. Type A people also crave information, so that we can always be ready with the right answer in any scenario.

Thus my need to know how to plan the perfect murder.


When you know your own tendencies, you can come up with workarounds to navigate daily life with fewer pitfalls. For example, I love reading magazines, but I've learned to save them for when I'm traveling. If I'm already stuck in an airport, it's not as much of a time loss when I blow an hour poring over pieces like "Nine Tips for a Stronger Golf Swing" and "Three Signs Your Cat May Be Depressed," which I shouldn't be reading anyway, because I don't golf or have a cat. Do I suspect someone's going to walk into a crowd and yell, "Help! My drives aren't making it down the fairway, and it's making my cat sad. What should I do?" and I'll be the one with the knowledge to save the day? I don't know. But that folly is best left for time that's already wasted.

I scrutinize minutiae as if I'm preparing for a test, and to me, everything in life is a test. Fill in the blank: The right job is _____. The right way to be a friend is _____. The right parenting style is _____. The right way to handle anxiety over whether or not I'm right about everything is _____.

This need to succeed comes out in silly ways—like when I take part in little private contests throughout the day, just so I can pat myself on the back: When I turn the page in a book, I give myself a split second to guess the first word on the next page. I also pretend there's an app in my bathroom mirror that's scoring me on how symmetrically I apply eyeliner to both eyes. I've done this stuff for as long as I can remember. As a kid, I ate my way around a plate as if someone might stop the clock any second and judge me based on how evenly I'd consumed the different food groups in my meal. (Three bites of egg, three bites of bagel, three bites of strawberry.) Teenage-me imagined I was being filmed in my closet, giving an interview about my organizational skills; I won imaginary prizes for keeping my shoes so neat. Dial back to any point on my timeline, and there I am, a contestant in a game show no one else can see.

I'm making it sound like being this way is fun, like it's a hilarious quirk, but to be clear: It's also miserable. I hate that I can't relax. I wish I didn't have a to-do list in my peripheral vision at all times.

It's an exhausting way to live, but try as I might, I can't turn it off. My brain seeks tasks to check off, i's to dot and t's to cross (not to mention x's to slash, e's to loop, and z's to zag), the way a sort-of-but-not-really reformed smoker sucks in a deep lungful of nicotine when walking past a crowd of smokers outside a bar. Like any high-functioning addict, I have learned to sneak a hit wherever I can. When the pediatrician gives me my kids' growth charts, I look for the percentages first. When the water meter guy handed me a report with our latest meter reading, I scanned it for a score and asked, "Is this good?" I can sustain a buzz for hours after anyone tells me that something I've done was "the best"—even if it's just a colleague at the bookstore where I work saying, "Hey, Mary Laura, you're the best at changing the toilet paper roll in the employee bathroom." *Bam.* Better than a shot of tequila.

Vacations are difficult to settle into when you're like this. A good day for me ends with completing something, looking at that thing all nice and finished, and letting a sense of accomplishment flood my nervous system. *Ahhhhh*, that's better. It soothes my mind and brings me peace—and peace is what vacation is supposed to be all about, right? But whip out a laptop at the pool, and people go nuts. *Workaholic*, they call you. *OCD. Control freak.* On my fortieth-birthday beach trip,

I hid in a cabana bathroom to finish edits on an article I was working on. There was no way I could enjoy a margarita until the assignment was complete.

I hear people talk about how fun it is to "do nothing" when they're off work, and I think, *I want to do nothing, too.* "Nothing" sounds wonderful. So I study how to be unstudied. I watch how laid-back people act and try to mimic it. I toss my purse on the floor and fling my arm breezily over the side of a chair, like I'm so relaxed I don't even care where my limbs or belongings land. Sometimes I can almost convince myself I feel it.

Luckily, one of my responsibilities at the bookstore is reading manuscripts of forthcoming books. That means that on vacation I can imitate relaxing while I'm actually working. All I have to do is lean back in my beach lounger and point to my stack of books and say, "Behold this leisurely reading I'm doing while casually wearing a sarong, free of all cares and work-related thoughts," when in fact I'm thinking, *Four books in three days. Yessss.*

If success came in snortable form, I'd sniff it up each nostril and rub the residue on my gums.

People like me—people who don't just enjoy being right, but *need* to be right—are often described as ballbusters, as if all we want in the world is to make everyone's lives harder. As if we take some pleasure in grinding our gears over every little problem in the world. Let me speak for my people and say, no, it's not that. I don't want to make anyone's life more difficult.

And I don't mean to come across as impatient, but I do like to be on time. I sense the ticking of an invisible stopwatch in everything I do, because life's to-do list never seems to get shorter, which means the only hope for feeling some sense of progress is to get through it without delay. My senior yearbook quote was, "Dost thou love life? Then do not squander time, for that is the stuff life is made of," by Benjamin Franklin. (So, so cool next to everyone else's Prince lyrics.)

It's Mr. Franklin's philosophy I always have in mind whenever people I have plans with are running late. I used to text them:

Are you coming?
Need me to pick you up?
Reservation in five mins.
Should I call and change it?

I sent a string of texts like this to a friend once. Then I noticed that after her *leaving soon* response to my first message, she had stopped answering. She pulled into my driveway to pick me up (for another friend's birthday dinner, for which we were now half an hour late), and when I opened the passenger door, she snapped, "I *know*."

She backed out of my driveway, looking in the rearview mirror, refusing to make eye contact with me. We sat silently side by side for the ride, and when we arrived at the restaurant, she leapt from the car as if being freed from a broken elevator, hustling over to where our other friends stood leisurely chatting near the door. No one had told the hostess our party was

23

late. No one had checked to see if the table was still available. Why was she so happy to see these irresponsible friends who didn't even care about making sure our dinner plan didn't fall apart? I was the one who'd tried to help her be on time. I was the one who'd tried to make everything right. And now she was mad at me!

I'd been freaking out because our plans had gone off the rails and I wanted to fix them. And yes, also because lateness makes me insane. But I realized as my friend gave an exasperated sigh and handed me a drink from the bar—an act I recognized in that moment as one of forgiveness—that she'd been more irritated by my prodding than she was frustrated by our scrambled plans or sorry about being late. I had made her feel rushed and belittled. When we were finally seated, another half hour later, the glow of our tabletop candlelight camouflaged how red my face had flushed with embarrassment.

I resolved, silently, to be less terrible next time.

Shortly thereafter, I started training myself not to text every hurry-up-where-are-you that popped into my head, thereby making me seem more relaxed. It's a front, but it preserves friendships.

I don't want people to feel I'm judging them. I don't want to be perceived as hostile, although I know that I sometimes am. But I'm not hostile like a crazy person punching strangers on a subway platform. I'm just hostile like a crazy person who wants to gouge her eyes out when she sees grammatical errors on billboards. LOWEST PRICE'S—I can hardly stand it.

My mind seeks the tidiness of a question answered. An agenda complete. A box checked. That's what harmony feels like in my brain. Wasted time and wrong answers disrupt that harmony like an off-key instrument making a dissonant clang in a musician's ears.

I'm not a monster. I just want everything to be perfect. Is that so much to ask?

(It's an icicle, by the way. The perfect murder weapon. It melts—no fingerprints!)

# Wonder Woman

**People** blame their parents for their flaws and eccentricities all the time. In interviews, in therapy, in memoirs, they enumerate the many ways their mothers fucked them up. It seems we can't discuss the way we are without assigning some responsibility to the generation before. Anyone can do it.

Chapel Hill, North Carolina. I was in first grade. My mother picked me up from school in our family Buick, as always. My dad, still in the early years of his medical career, was off working at the hospital most of the time, so the role of daily caretaker fell to her, as it did with most mothers then. She had been a schoolteacher before we were born—me, then my brother— and once she had us, she stayed home and we became her tiny class of two. When we were little, she was the one human being we saw most. She was our guide to how the world worked, not to mention our food source, our referee, our correctional officer, our chief entertainer—the de facto center of our universe.

That afternoon, I unloaded my Wonder Woman book bag onto the vinyl bench seat of our car and showed my mother the stack of papers we'd all been sent home with, a list of words printed on each page. Easy ones like *love*, *candy*, *bike*, and harder ones like *breath*, *power*, and *understand*. That week there was to be a spelling contest, winnowing the class down to the best spellers, ultimately crowning a champion.

Later that evening and every night that week, after my brother had been put to bed, she sat at one end of our green chenille sofa and I sat at the other as she called out two pages' worth of words for me to spell aloud. I flailed around on the cushions, impatient, wanting to get down and read a book. "Why two?" I whined. "The teacher said one page a day." My mom—in the same matter-of-fact tone she used for important edicts such as *Stay out of the street*; *Eat your fruit*; *Go back and brush those teeth again, they're still yellow*—said, "Always do more than expected. That's how you win."

That's how you win.

By the time the spelling bee started on Monday, I was ready. I moved on to the next round and did it all again on Tuesday, then Wednesday, then Thursday. When Friday came, sure enough, I clinched that contest. I don't remember if I got a medal or whether the other kids high-fived me, but I can vividly remember—as if she were standing in front of me right now—my mother's beaming face. She raised her eyebrows and nodded as she broke into a smile. She was *proud of me*, and I was the Wonder Woman of spelling.

Had the term existed back then, my mom probably would have been deemed a tiger mother. She taught my brother and me to read when each of us were three, starting us out with *Hop on Pop* and *Go, Dog, Go!* In second grade, she offered me a

Rubik's Cube if I could ace my multiplication tables before the class deadline. In middle school, she woke us up every weekday at 5:45 a.m. to practice our piano. She never used cruelty—we weren't chained in a cellar practicing fractions, although our protests may have sounded like we were. But through repeated practice, she made it clear that we were not fully prepared until we were *overprepared*, and that the desired goal, the *only* goal, was an A. Nobody makes a B in this house.

It was a simple rule—"work first, play later"—and it taught me that the natural order of things was to study hard, achieve your goal and receive the approval of your loved ones, and then (but not a minute before) relax.

We weren't a family who held hands during the blessing or told each other we loved each other out loud, but the look on my mother's face when I showed her an A+ said, "I love you."

Good grades gave me evidence that, at least until the next test, I was secure in my place as a preferred person in my house and in my school and—probably, why not?—in the world. Naturally it stood to reason that the opposite was true as well. I remember the times I didn't make good grades. There was a decimals test in fourth grade. After we got it back, everyone had to get it signed. I held it out to my mom, searching her face for a reaction as she put her signature on the page right next to the dreaded *80*, feeling in my gut the absence of her smile. It was the absence of the ground beneath my feet. I may not have grasped decimals perfectly, but I could do this reverse calculation: If an A means *You are loved and you belong here*, then anything less than an A must mean *You are not and you don't.*

When you internalize what you believe to be someone else's opinion of you, it becomes *your* opinion of you.

I came to rely on grades for my regular jolt of self-esteem. It's a miracle I didn't end up with a back injury from bringing all my books home every night in case I realized I needed to complete an extra assignment in something. It became my routine, one that lasted well past middle school into high school and even college, long after the days of bringing grades home for a signature: Study my ass off, panic that my run of luck was over and I'd fail, then get my grades back. The validation would rush to my head, a perfect high. Each hit set chaos into order. Every check mark, every gold star, confirmed it: *I succeed, therefore I am.*

Perhaps this is why misspelled words cause me a disproportionate amount of rage to this day. When I see *mischievous* spelled *mischeivious* I don't just think, *Hey, that's wrong*, I think, *WHERE IS THAT WRITER'S SELF-RESPECT?* Somewhere inside my brain, first-grade-me is also wondering, aghast, *Don't you want to be loved?*

I had a freelance editing client years ago, a CEO who'd been at her job for decades. She refused to accept my edits whenever I removed the double spaces she placed after periods at the ends of sentences. Again and again, I'd strip out the extra spaces and send her documents back with single spaces, and she'd add the spaces back in. That was what she'd learned in school, she insisted. I'd get purple in the face explaining that, yes, double spaces were required back in the day when everyone used typewriters but that modern word-processing programs had rendered obsolete the manual widening of the space between sentences. One space was the new rule. "Don't you want to be *right*?" I'd say, exasperated. "I *am* right," she'd say. Maybe we were too much alike, an impossible match.

I worry that my kids will inherit my worst traits, that they'll turn out too much like me, fixated on racing to the finish line with a perfect score. So when they walk through the door in the afternoons these days, I ask them what they had for lunch. I don't actually care what they ate. I mean, I do—I'm their mother, so of course I'm concerned that they're working their way around the food pyramid or the food train or whatever it is now. The lunch question is about something else.

I'd be thrilled if my kids made the dean's list, and you better believe I make them learn those extra spelling words. But I also want my daughter to try a risky science experiment, and when it goes differently than expected, I want her to shrug it off and try another one. I want my son to bring home paintings and clay sculptures he's proud of because they're beautiful in his own eyes, not because they got him a good grade.

So I don't ask them about their grades the minute they come home. Silently, I give myself an A+ for this move. I award myself an invisible certificate of achievement for parenting excellence, with high honors in nurturing a value system that emphasizes effort and curiosity over quantification. I do that because over in a little corner of my head, six-year-old-me

31

sits on a big green sofa, clutching her spelling pages, wanting desperately to hear, *Good job*. She never left; she'll never leave. It's too late for her, but not for them. They can be better than I am.

Maybe they'll grow up to have a strange obsession with lunch and blame me.

So there you have it.

When I was growing up, my mother was a hard-ass, and she turned me compulsive.

It's all my mother's fault.

Or:

When I was growing up, my mother was my cheerleader, and she made me successful.

It's all to my mother's credit.

Chapel Hill. First grade. My mom picked me up from school. Left to my own devices, I might have crammed those spelling pages back into the bottom of my book bag with the empty, peanut-butter-smeared sandwich baggies and the balled-up sweatshirt I hadn't worn in a month.

But my mother intervened and changed everything. She had seen how quickly I took to books, how I'd sit and read, focusing until I got to the end of a story. She had noticed how naturally I recalled a word once I'd seen it a single time. She saw potential I could not have seen in myself at that age. She reached for that stack of spelling words.

And so my brother was sent to bed while I was allowed to stay up. I got to snuggle into the nubby pillows of the green sofa next to my mom as I learned tricks for training my brain to hold as much as it could. I found that if you spell a word out loud five times in a row, the sixth time is a snap.

"Hair. H-a-i-r. Hair," I spelled.

"Yes!" she cried.

I started spelling words in conversation: "I'm going o-u-t-s-i-d-e now." "Do I have to wash my f-a-c-e tonight?" My mother showed me how to bump up against what felt like the natural limits of my mind and then keep pushing into the territory that lay beyond.

When I won that spelling bee, I got a smile from my mom that no one else got. This wasn't just regular love like all parents had for their kids. This was extra love, something more, just for me. It filled me up, and I would never again settle for anything less.

When I held out my math test with a B on it, she didn't reward me with a smile, because she believed I could have made an A. In time, *I* believed I could make A's, too. She held me to the standards she knew I could meet. As if running alongside my bike with a hand on my seat, then letting go, she guided me until I could excel on my own.

My work ethic helped me earn my way into opportunities that changed my life: contests, college, jobs, assignments. I became a person other people can count on, someone they trust to do a good job. I grew to think of myself this way, as a helpful person, a reliable person.

My mother the wonder woman made me a wonder woman, too.

Even small events can have a formative effect on our lives. Everything sinks into the soil.

That's how I think of that first-grade spelling bee. Did it really change me from one kind of person into another? I suspect it was less a cause of my perfectionism than simply the first manifestation of it, but I remember it as a before-and-after marker on my timeline. My best guess is that something within me, some strand of DNA, was extra susceptible to the idea of quantifiable self-worth, and school was the perfect environment for it to thrive. (Seriously: a spelling bee for *first graders*? The 1980s were hard-core.) Plenty of other kids had strict parents, too, but they didn't all become obsessive about grades. My brother grew up right alongside me, but when he got a B, he just went into his room and played his Bon Jovi tapes. Big deal.

Of all the genes parents pass down and values they instill, how does one take hold so much stronger than the others? How do two kids with the same genetic ingredients and upbringing turn into such different people? My brother became a high-achieving student, too, but also a sneaky, laid-back teenager, the kid who hid beer in our backyard tree house and laughed it off when he got caught. I became uptight and anxious, the one who religiously performed all three steps of the Clinique three-step cleansing system every night because the instructions said, *Wash, tone, moisturize.* He stood right next to me when my mother said, "Practice your piano for thirty minutes each while I'm at the grocery store." So why did I slog through half an hour of Beethoven every time and then watch in fuming rage as he played video games? Does it even matter why?

There's not much I'd blame any parent for, honestly, now that I am one. Cruelty, neglect, abuse—absolutely—but word-drilling on the green sofa? No. We're all a little weird thanks to our mothers. I'm carrying that tradition on with my own children.

What a job, to raise someone from birth to adulthood, bestowing upon them your knowledge and your values and, despite your best intentions, any number of traits you've inherited yourself. What a loaded task, to make every move, every day, in such a way that the impressionable larva-person in your home will see your example, process it into something within herself, and grow layers of muscle and soul over it until she is a fully developed human being. And all the while, the little person you're nurturing is fighting you—spitting out the broccoli, not wearing the helmet, rolling her eyes at your carefully chosen words of advice—and you become constantly worn down even as you pour your energies into loving her.

My mom gave me all the tools she had, some of which I couldn't use. She grew up to be a plant whisperer after helping her dad tend his garden in the wild green lot behind their little house outside Birmingham, Alabama, and she tried to teach me to be one, too. I used to follow her around our backyard, watching her reach into a mass of stems and leaves with her clippers and snip this bloom or that one to toss into her basket; then I'd sit mesmerized as she stuck them into vases and bowls, creating what looked like tabletop parade floats. She'd coach me to do the same—"Here, put some greenery in, make it look softer"—and I'd stab a branch into the bunch, ruining the loose beauty of her arrangement. You point to anything with roots, and she can name it, arrange it, and/or cook it, and I can't keep a pot of basil alive for longer than a week. Why didn't *that* stick?

What did stick—whether she intended to pass it along or not—was her sense of humor. When it came to academics, my mom may have been a warlord zipped into the body of Sally Field, but the rest of the time, she cracked us up. Whenever a Little Richard song came on the car radio, she would bust a move at the wheel like a one-woman episode of *Dance Fever*. She let me play beauty salon and make dozens of tiny pigtails all over her head with my colorful plastic barrettes. When I was bothered by the fact that none of my Barbies had underwear, she sewed a complete trousseau of tiny lingerie. Like her, I love little visual absurdities (ah, the inherent hilarity of a teeny-weeny doll bra), dry one-liners and well-timed cracks, and perfectly executed, utterly insane mishmashes of curse words. (My mom, upon walking into a messy room: "It looks like the ass end of destruction in here." The ass end of destruction!)

When I was seventeen, I might have told you I was a neurotic student because my mom was so tough about grades. When I was twenty-five, I might have shrugged and said, eh, maybe it was my mom who made me a control freak or maybe

I'm just me, who knows. By the time I reached my thirties and had my own children, I knew perfect parenting was a myth, and I understood that while she was responsible for making me, she couldn't have known how I'd end up made. No one could have. That's a little mystery we all unfurl on our own.

# Lobsterman

**Each** time I wedge myself into a tiny chair at a lima bean–shaped table for another parent-teacher conference, I remind myself not to panic. Whatever the teacher reports my offspring have gotten up to lately, I probably did something similar as a kid, and I turned out okay.

In kindergarten, I got in trouble for scribbling little hatch marks on the sides of my worksheets—not once, not twice, but again and again. Whenever I completed my subtraction or my fill-in-the-blanks, I began graying in one corner of the paper with my pencil, methodically covering the page in lines until the whole thing was unreadable. The teacher brought my mom in and asked me in front of her, "Why, Mary Laura? Why won't you stop?" To which I replied, "I don't know."

I was confused. Why did it matter? I'd done my worksheets. The answers were right. So I wanted to do some shading while I waited for everyone else—why the fuss?

She continued, "If you don't stop, you'll have to skip art." I stopped for a day or two, then started again. It seemed so harmless. So I found myself sitting alone, banished to a little table where I would, supposedly, sit and think about curbing my scribbling habit. My friend Cynthia sneaked me balls of Play-Doh, and I mashed them against the underside of the table into blue and green and pink pancakes.

Once I was allowed back from exile, I quit scribbling on my papers, but I never did understand what the big deal was.

My third-grade teacher reprimanded me almost daily for writing in phrases instead of sentences. We had to read these little paragraphs—"Mike drives a bus in the morning. The bus is red. Children get on. Children get off." And then we were expected to answer questions about them in complete sentences.

But tell me this: If someone asked you, "What does Mike drive?" would you say, *Mike drives a red bus?* Or would you say, *A red bus?* I bet you'd say, *A red bus.* Otherwise, you're wasting words, right? No sense being redundant. Alas, my teacher did not agree. I got an F in writing, but I stand by those sentence fragments. Economy of words.

(You'd think an F would have really set me off. But unlike a B, which means you haven't quite achieved an A, an F seemed like a crazy novelty, not even a real grade. "That woman's an idiot," my mom said.)

I learned how to write in complete sentences—I'd known how all along, really—and I started using them at school, but only when I had to.

In seventh grade, we were instructed to keep a journal for two weeks. We could "journal" (as a verb) about anything at all, the teacher said. Anything! The point was to write every day. So for two weeks over Christmas break, I chronicled the plot of every episode of *The Young and the Restless*. When we returned to school and took turns reading our journals aloud, everyone read about their feelings and their daily activities. I read about how Nikki and Victor were fighting again and no one knew if Danny and Cricket would ever get back together.

My classmates laughed (which I liked) and said, "I can't believe you wrote that" (which I didn't like so much). Why couldn't they believe it? We were allowed to write anything, right? Why was my thing weird? For that matter, why didn't anyone else write about TV?

In eleventh grade, my English teacher gave our class a pop writing assignment in which we were to write a story that began with the sentence she wrote on the board. The sentence was something like, "The lobsterman looked out over the water." I don't recall exactly, but the word *lobsterman* was definitely in there. I remember thinking really hard about this character and what a difficult life he must have being half man, half lobster.

He's the most human-like of the monsters, and the most monstrous of quasi-humans. He walks on two legs and doesn't have superpowers. He can't shoot flames from his eyes or breathe underwater. He is almost totally normal, as people go, but for that one little thing. . . . Where other people have fingers, which they use to hold on to coffee cups, to wave in greeting, to clasp each other in love, he has a hard, sharp pincer that would crush human bones if he tried to shake hands. He wears oversize sleeves sometimes, so his difference isn't always immediately noticeable, but everyone figures it out eventually.

He can't carry open-weave crocheted shopping bags. The holes catch his claws and snag. He has lost too many groceries this way, oranges and cans of crabmeat rolling across the sidewalk.

But on the upside, he can remove the crimped metal tops from beer bottles without a bottle opener.

He sunburns easily.

He has a real name, maybe Melvin or Jake, but no one remembers what it is because everyone around town calls him Lobsterman, but only behind his back, because most people don't talk to him at all.

Poor Lobsterman. Out there living among regular men with regular hands. Misunderstood. Impaired. Shunned.


I found out after turning in the paper that a lobsterman is a person who catches lobsters, like a fisherman. How did all my classmates know that? We lived nowhere near the water.


When my son was three, my spouse and I sat at another lima bean as his preschool teacher told us that he was failing to complete tasks that involved cutting, because he was unable to hold a pair of scissors. She asked why we hadn't taught him this basic skill. "Wait," I said, "aren't we supposed to be keeping sharp things *away* from him?"

I thought I'd been such a good parent, creating a safe, blade-free environment for my toddler. The other parents were teaching their little ones to cut, I guess, while I was snapping up all the scissors in the house, going, "Nope, not for you!" Why didn't I know?

In school we're taught to do our best, but we're limited by the bounds of what we understand to be right—and "right" looks different to everyone, apparently. Maybe we all walk around assuming everyone is interpreting the world the same way we are, and being surprised when they aren't, and that's the loneliness and confusion of the human experience in a nutshell (er, lobster shell).

I wonder how many times my children will find themselves in a lobsterman-story scenario, where they're doing one thing only to find out later that everybody else was doing another? And how many of those will be because I lobstermanned something as a parent?

Quite a few, probably, and there's no way to see them coming. But tell me this: Which would you rather read—a story about a guy who catches lobsters or a story about a guy who *is* a lobster?

# Mermaids and Destiny

**Every** now and then, a school will ask me to come speak to a group of students, and each time I do it, I get a little nervous. I always wonder what I might possibly have to say that teenagers want to hear. When I ask teachers what they expect me to talk about, they say, "Tell them about your life path, your career." I suppose this is because the job market is garbage these days and kids need to know there are lots of ways to make a living, even by cobbling together a hodgepodge of part-time jobs and creative projects. Maybe they want students to see that if their real dreams don't work out, they can always draw cartoons. I'm not sure, but I want to prove myself worthy of the invitation, so I try to leave them with something useful.

I start by showing a picture of myself in second grade: In the photo, I'm caught mid-jump, throwing a basketball that's clearly headed about two feet short of the basket. I'm wearing soccer cleats (to play *basketball*) with a T-shirt tucked snugly into the elastic waist of my shorts, just under my armpits. I'm grinning like I think I'm really nailing it, and my hair is tied with white bows in two pigtails.

"You might look at this and assume I'd grow up to be a

professional athlete," I begin. "But life doesn't always turn out the way you expect." Gets a laugh every time.

Whether you think you know exactly who you'll become or you have absolutely no idea, I tell them, one thing is true for everyone, for better or for worse: Life will surprise you. You'll hit dead-ends and detours. There will be times when you can't fathom what comes next. When that happens, remember yourself as you are right now. Remember yourself as you were when you were even younger. Who were you when you weren't wondering who you were?

Here's who I was.

I was seven, I was bored, and I had already pillaged our living room bookshelves for everything except the Sidney Sheldon and Danielle Steel, which I couldn't reach. So I grabbed what was left: a dusty, leather-bound book of short stories by Hans Christian Andersen. It fell open to "The Little Mermaid."

This was the first I had heard of mermaids (the book came into my life before the movie), and the opening conversation between a bevy of teenage mermaid sisters and their grandmother hooked me immediately. The youngest sister, who has just witnessed a shipwreck and helped a drowning human prince to shore, wants to know: How long do humans live? How long do mermaids live? What happens when you die? (You can see how it appealed to a seven-year-old.)

Mermaids, according to the grandmother, live for three hundred years. Humans live a shorter time, but when they die, their souls live on forever. Not so for mermaids. "Is there anything I can do to get an immortal soul?" the mermaid asks. Not much, the grandmother answers. You'd have to marry a human, but that's darn near impossible, because mermaids can't walk on land. Tough tail-fins, sister.

Among the many ways the original short story differs from the cartoon film (see also: singing crabs, oyster-shell bikinis), there is one whopper of a distinction, and you get a hint of it in this line: "She could not forget the charming prince, nor her sorrow that she had not an immortal soul like his." See, in the story, the little mermaid thinks the prince is cute, but she doesn't decide to go back out to the beach looking for him because he's so irresistible. She goes back because she wants a soul.

The way I read it, she's not lovesick. She's ambitious.

But to get what she wants, she has to strike a raw deal with a bad witch and trade away her voice for feet. Then everything goes wrong. Once on land, she can't tell anyone who she is or what she needs—she can't say anything—and she ends up standing mutely by as the prince meets and marries someone else. The real bummer is that, according to the witchy bargain, she can't cut her losses, grow her tail back, and revert to mermaid life. Failing to seal the deal means she is doomed to die. After the prince and his new bride are married on the deck of a grand ship, the mermaid-turned-human stays up all night gazing out at the waves because she knows she won't live past sunrise. Then, just before morning, she sees her sisters rise to the surface, waving frantically.

It turns out that in this bizarre underwater commerce where you can buy magic with your body parts, they've traded their long, beautiful seaweed hair for one last out. There's a way the little mermaid can save herself: "The witch has given us a knife," they say. "Before the sun rises, you must plunge it into the heart of the prince. When his warm blood falls upon your feet, they will grow together again, and you will once more be a mermaid. Or in a few minutes the sun will rise, and you must die."

Kill or be killed. Your classic Scylla and Charybdis, the devil and the deep blue sea. That's a bit darker than the animated movie.

The little mermaid takes the knife. She sneaks into the ship's honeymoon suite. She raises the blade over the sleeping prince, poised to stab him . . . and she can't do it. She drops the knife and leaves the room, then slips over the rail of the ship and into the water, where she dissolves into sea foam. She has lost her remaining 285 mermaid years; she has lost her brief humanity; and, most tragically, she has lost what she gambled everything for—a chance at a soul. It's all over.


Holy hammerheads, that story made me mad. I read and reread it until my thumbs wore the print off the pages, desperate to find the loophole, some way it could all end differently. What could the mermaid have done to turn things around, to get everyone's attention and explain herself before it was too late? I mean, good grief, couldn't she have written a simple note?

My God, couldn't she?

I obsessed over this fictional dilemma for years. As unlikely as it may seem that a seven-year-old would fall asleep raging against Neptune, plotting undersea education reform, I was stuck on it. I couldn't decide whom I was angrier at: the fictional mermaid population for not developing some sort of alphabet or sign language, or Hans Christian Andersen for leaving such a ridiculous hole in the story. It was so unfair—so *stupid*—that the sea-girl couldn't write her way out of trouble.

When I think about that mermaid now, I think about the things people trade away to get something else.

I think about what other girls suffer, girls who live not under the sea, but in places where the deck is stacked against females from the start, cities where it's not safe to walk to school, countries where young women are forced to marry against their will. I think of the lengths some women must go to in order to protect their own lives. I think about my daughter, my friends' daughters, girls growing up in America at a time when the word *feminist* is fashionable again, and girls growing up in places where feminism has not even broken through to the surface.

I think about people who can't ask for what they need, and also people who just think they can't. I think about how sometimes we hesitate to speak up out of fear of being seen as selfish or greedy. Imagine the lives we'd live if we were all able to say what we wanted out loud, or put it on paper if necessary.

And as I reflect on my imaginary mermaid friend who lacked the skills to save herself, I also think about what that story taught me—and I don't mean the contrived moral tacked onto the end of the fairy tale; I mean the lesson I took away from it and carried with me forever.

Baby, you better learn to write.

---

This is the story I tell when the students ask, "Did you always know you'd be a writer?" It's my way of saying, "On some level, yes." Did I always love books? Sure. Did I always ruminate on the strange details of what I read? Definitely. Has it always seemed vitally important that I find a way to express what I'm thinking, as if to fail to let my thoughts out of my head would kill me just like it killed that mermaid? Yeah, kind of.

But I give a warning, too. When people tell stories about their childhood as a way of prophesying what they'd become as adults, be suspicious. Nobody's path is as linear as it looks in retrospect. Did the famous TV chef really know she had a future in pastry making after eating a cupcake when she was four? Or is she now a baker who happens to remember eating a cupcake? She probably did a lot of other things as a kid, too. Maybe she was on a kickball team in second grade, but she's not a professional kickballer now, is she? I went through a phase for about three years where I spent every afternoon coasting around my neighborhood on my bike, but I'm not a biker today. I don't even have a bike. Contrary to the old aphorism, I'm pretty sure I've forgotten how to ride one.

The picture you get at the end of a connect-the-dots activity really depends on which dots you decide to use. So try things and go through phases. Put down a lot of dots. Later, you can look back and pick any of those dots to create a picture of how you became who you are. And if you don't like the picture you end up with, you can always choose different dots, which just goes to show destiny isn't all it's cracked up to be.

# Disappearing Act

**It** starts the same way every time. An invisible, icy finger plucks my spine like a harp string, and a vibration begins at the back of my skull. The cold spreads up into my head and down into my limbs. My breaths become shallow, and what I suddenly want most is one big gulp of fresh air. People who witness it say it happens in a flash, that I stumble and crumple before they can reach me, but to me it feels like slow motion, a cartoonish antigravity spacewalk. A few seconds balloon into a suspended moment, then the shutoff valve is tripped. My eyes close, and I'm out, as if asleep. Splat.

No matter how many variables you introduce into my life—location, age, situation—one thing that remains is my habit of dropping out of consciousness without notice. Same face-plant, different floor.

I once fainted in my bathroom, the hair dryer still dangling from its cord, twirling and blowing hot air as I lay on the tile. Another time, as a kid, I fainted in church while wearing a heavy linen robe, just after handing off my big candle to another acolyte. I fainted in high school with some regularity. On one occasion, the buzz crept into my head during our pig dissection in biology; I set down my tools, stepped away from the lab desk, and put my hands out to protect my face before the world went dark. I once slid down the wall of a hallway in an academic building in college; my humanities professor saw it happen, and when I woke up, he half dragged me to a quieter hallway, where I sat until I felt ready to walk again. A few years after that, I passed out face-first onto a newspaper and stood up a few minutes later with backward headlines on my cheek. I've fainted at various workplaces through the years, although it probably always looked like I was napping, my head resting on crossed arms upon my desk.

Every time I faint—either as I'm going down or when I'm waking up—I have a split-second flashback to the first time, in kindergarten. It was morning sing-along. I had started feeling spacey during the Pledge of Allegiance, and by the time we wrapped up liberty and justice for all, my face, hands, and feet had turned cold, and my classmates' voices had faded into the ringing inside my head. The distance between me and everyone around me stretched out, distorted by the suddenly too-thin air. Having never experienced this before, I fought it. I tried to stay standing.

(We were about to sing "The Farmer in the Dell," you see, and it was Mike C.'s turn to be the farmer, which meant that when we got to the "farmer takes a wife" verse, he'd have to pick a girl, and the hell if I was going to let him pick that Missy girl again, because she eats erasers, and—)

*Thud.*

I can't stop it once it starts.

This type of fainting—"syncope" if you like fancy medical words, "swooning" if you live in 1870 and wear a corset—is not uncommon. It occurs because my blood isn't rushing through my veins so much as it's just drifting along like the lazy-river raft ride. Sometimes the oxygenated blood doesn't make it all the way up to my head, so down I go. If I could control it, it would make a great party trick (*Watch this! Boom*), but alas, I cannot. I've grown accustomed to it, though. The only thing it has really cost me is any hope of a career as a surgeon. Or a pilot. Or a stripper, I guess. Anything where reliable motor control and maintaining consciousness is important.

Repeat experience taught me an important lesson: The second I feel it coming on is the instant to stop whatever I'm doing and move as close to the ground as possible. If I get myself ready to fall, I won't drop as far or as hard. Preparation is protection.

If fainting was one recurring experience in my young life, the other was moving. Because my dad was working on his medical specialty, neuro-otology, he had to do a new fellowship every few years. When he did, off we went to another town with a teaching hospital. The legs of our furniture always had orange stickers left on them by various movers. I'd pick at them with my thumbnail. *Allied. United.* Numbers to match the table to the truck.

Fainting and uprooting. I never knew when they'd happen, only that they would. My world could disappear without notice, and there was nothing I could do about it.

———

I was born in Nashville when my dad was a resident at Vanderbilt University. My brother was born when we lived in Hagerstown, Maryland, outside Washington, DC. We lived in Nashville again briefly before moving to Chapel Hill, North Carolina, which is where I started school. At age three, I went to a progressive preschool in a tree house out in the woods, where we were encouraged to wander in nature and finger paint on easels propped in pine straw. The next year I started kindergarten at a regular school (one with walls, where I first went down) in town.

I don't remember being told that we had to move from North Carolina, but at some point in the summer after first grade, we ended up at a rental house in the suburbs of Memphis. When second grade started, I enrolled in school and made a best friend named Erica. Over the winter break, we moved from the suburbs into Memphis proper, and I went back to second grade after Christmas at a different school. I never saw Erica again. At my new school, everyone knew each other. Everyone but me.

I made another new best friend—a few of them, actually: one who loved her sticker album as much as I treasured mine and was willing to trade scratch-and-sniffs to fill out our collections, and another who lived down the street and could walk to my house, where we sang along to her mother's Barry Manilow cassettes on my front porch using sticks as microphones. My family stayed in that house longer than we had stayed anywhere before. As years passed, my friends and I grew from little kids to preteens. We had fights and fell out, then got back together.

When my mother told me we had to move again, I was in seventh grade. I should have seen it coming but I didn't. I took it hard. We stood in front of the fireplace in our den, and she began, "We've always thought we might have one more move . . ." as I nodded, thinking, *Unfair, unfair, unfair.* I'd thought Memphis was it, our final home, the place we got to stay. I'd thought these were the friends I'd get to keep. Later, I found an index card on which she'd written notes: "Always thought—one more."

I cried about that move. I resented having to leave Memphis. But I also knew I had no control over the situation. I went to the goodbye parties my friends threw me, and we took Polaroids of each other to keep as mementos, but at no point did I throw a fit or scream, "I'm not going!" Like a fainting spell, it was going to happen whether I fought it or not. Might as well accept it and go peacefully.

In Memphis, I once fainted while my grandmother was visiting from Alabama. She called it "the vapors." *She's got the vapors,* she said. I didn't know that was an old-timey term for fainting, so I was confused. I hadn't smelled anything before I blacked out. What vapors?

My parents said Augusta, Georgia, the town where my father had grown up, was the right place for him to start his own medical practice at last, but I couldn't picture living there. I knew it only from visiting my grandparents during the Masters golf tournament once every few years. We had taken road trips there, when my brother and I would splash around in my grandparents' pool with the children of my father's five younger siblings. As the oldest of all the cousins, I often got bored hanging out with the little kids, and I'd wander upstairs to find my grandfather's collection of Stephen King paperbacks.

When we arrived in Augusta that summer, my mother arranged an introduction to two girls my age. She dropped me off at the Augusta Mall, and I soon found myself sitting with two strangers before a slice of greasy pizza too large for its paper plate. After lunch, we cruised the department store perfume counters, spritzing and waving. Should we go to Banana Republic? Oh, definitely. You like belts? I like belts! Maybe things wouldn't be so bad.

Things were fine.

I fainted in Augusta with some regularity. I once fainted in my room while I was doing homework, *smack* right onto my algebra. When I woke up, I went into the bathroom and looked in the mirror. My face looked like wax, white and shiny.

After making it through high school, I selected Davidson College in North Carolina with all the anywhere-but-here intention of a senior who's just ready to get out. But once I got there, I imprinted on it like a baby duck. I had attended six different schools growing up—none of which I chose—but this one was mine. This town was mine. These people were mine. The modular bed/desk/wardrobe/loft combo in the dorm room I shared with a soft-spoken anthropology major from South Carolina was mine. I made the best friends of my life, and although we all knew it would be over in four years, at least *we all knew*. It wasn't just me who would have to leave. Everyone would be shaken back out into the world at the same time, and until then, we were in this together.

I once fainted in the hallway between my dorm room and the hall bathroom while wearing a towel. Another time, I fainted while getting dressed and hit my head on a chair, giving myself a goose egg I had to explain for a week.

The further I get into adulthood, the less it has happened. I've never fainted while driving. When I became a new mother, I used to wonder what would happen if it ever occurred when I was at home alone with the children. It did, once, and as it turns out, they saw Mom's sudden nap as a great opportunity to get into the pantry and gorge themselves on salty pretzels and powdery mini-marshmallows.

I still think of fainting when I think about moving, and not just because I fainted everywhere I lived. Neurologists say that repeating the same thought patterns or behaviors over time can create mental pathways your brain automatically takes in the future. If the pattern persists long enough, it forges a circuit in your mind that becomes hardwired. This makes perfect sense when I consider how many of my behaviors as an adult come from patterns set years ago: I brush my teeth starting with the back upper-left teeth, then upper-right, then lower-left, then lower-right, then front. Always the same. If you made me do it in a different order, it would feel like writing with my left hand.

I'm no brain doctor, but I suspect that just as my body developed a go-to response to a drop in blood pressure, my mind came to expect a certain routine: Move somewhere, get used to it, then go somewhere else. I think that's why later, after spending several years in one place, I got antsy to move, although there were other reasons, too.

I do know that learning to give in to sudden fainting spells and weathering the end of friendships severed by childhood moves gave me practice in accepting, without struggle, the unexpected. Don't make a big deal, let it pass, everything's fine.

# P-O-I-S-O-N

I was living away from home for the first time. This meant I was doing a lot of things simply because they were not what I would have done under my parents' roof. Getting haircuts that were bold but not particularly flattering. Wearing crop tops that left my belly chilled by an uncomfortable breeze. Eating cereal and drinking Coke and calling it dinner, not because it made me feel good, but because I could. Because no one could stop me. I was defiantly, absurdly, the boss of myself.

It was also the early 1990s, which means I was emerging into the world having been fed a diet of late-'80s television. If there was a theme to TV relationships back then, it was *painful longevity*. Perhaps I'd taken in too many seasons of *Thirtysomething* or too many afternoons of *The Oprah Winfrey Show*, but I had it in my head that the whole point of a grown-up relationship was to take on life's rocky obstacles and work things out, episode after episode. This made sense to my goal-oriented mindset. If success at a task came from effort, why would relationships be any different? It must be normal for love to require a lot of work.

---

Whenever talk among my friends turns to past relationships, it comes out that at some point everyone dated a person who was totally wrong but really fun for a little while.

I knew him socially. He was popular, loud, kind of a clown. Our mutual friends probably kept him around so they could enjoy watching his stunts without suffering the consequences of them. Someone might say, "I wonder what happens if you drink a whole bottle of mustard?" and he would pick up a bottle of French's and try it. He did spot-on impressions of rappers, presidents, radio commercials . . . you name it. He was human entertainment.

Perhaps I was drawn to him because he didn't fit the profile of anyone I dated before (or after, for that matter). In my short dating history thus far, I'd been with nice guys, friendly nerds. But when he hit on me at a party, he got my attention. No one had ever just grabbed my sleeve, pulled me over, and kissed me square on the lips before. I probably should have slugged him, but I was too naive to be anything but impressed. He knocked me off-kilter and made me see myself in a new way. Was I the kind of woman who inspired spontaneous kissing?

In retrospect, I picture tiny mythical creatures—fate fairies, you might say—buzzing around the two of us, trying to signal me. There they were, hovering over his head, crossing their arms in a "No!" gesture whenever I leaned toward him. They shook their wands in my face when I picked up the phone to call him. I believe we all have these little voices telling us what we *should* be doing (whether we call them fate fairies or something else), and when we're ready, we pay attention to them. But before we're ready, they might as well be mute. When they first showed up, I was deaf to their protests. I missed the signs.

There was the time he canceled our plans because he said he wasn't feeling well, so I went out with a girlfriend instead. On my way home, I passed his apartment, where he was having a party so huge, cars were parked on the sidewalk. That was a sign. When I expressed my disappointment that he had lied to me, he asked me why I was being such a nag. Instead of saying, "I'm not a nag, and you're an asshole," I said, "I don't know. Let's talk about it. We can work it out." That's what the dramatic heroines on TV would say.

Once, after we road-tripped to a concert, I found out that every time he got up from our seats, supposedly to go to the bathroom, he'd been going out to my car in the parking lot to sell LSD he'd hidden in my trunk. Another sign. A billboard, really. But I told myself that one was on me, because I had never actually communicated that I did *not* want to be a drug-running accomplice. Oprah always told couples having disagreements to use a "When you _____ / I feel _____" statement. I gave it a try in my head: "WHEN YOU hide drugs in my car and drive us across state lines, I FEEL nervous because that's a felony."

Every time these neon signs appeared, I doubled down on devotion. What I wanted was to get back to the parts of the relationship I did like—the jokes, the dinners, the walking around in public with a guy prone to yelling "I LOVE YOU!" aloud on a crowded sidewalk. So, while my friends went out and had fun, I'd sit on the same corner on my dorm bed for hours-long phone calls (a necessary form of communication in the pre-texting age), my back against the wall and my blue duvet pulled over my knees, saying things like, "I FEEL that you're not respecting me WHEN YOU say you'll call me at eight but you don't call until eleven the next day." He'd say, "Don't give up on us, we'll work on things," and I'd say, "Okay, let's *work on it*." And I'd cry. Then I'd keep crying. I swear if I saw that duvet right now, my eyes would well up.

When I look back at my young self all mixed up with this person who did not care if I got sad or hurt (or arrested), I feel for the fate fairies, and I can see the moment they said, "Oh, for fuck's sake," and pulled out all the stops. It was the night he came over and lifted his shirt to show me his giant new tattoo: P-O-I-S-O-N with a skull and crossbones.

Did I take the hint? I did not. This was my Very Adult Relationship and no one—no friend, no parent, no symbol inked on skin—could talk me into letting it go. I was not going to fail at it. "Can you believe this shit?" the fate fairies must have said to one another, throwing up their hands.

After we'd been dating several months, I had to leave the country. The British literature program I had enrolled in months earlier was already arranged and paid for, and there was no changing it. Oh, the delicious drama of departure. A long-distance relationship was going to take *so* much work. It would all hinge on good communication, Oprah said. After some tearful (on my part) farewells by airport pay phone, I boarded my flight to London.

I took the train to Cambridge University, where I moved into a two-hundred-year-old cottage I was to share with eight other young women. I couldn't bring my blue duvet or many of my things from home, just a suitcase full of cotton clothes insufficient for the cold, damp weather. At a shop in town, I tried on woolly scarves and heavy sweaters, regarding my bundled-up self in a dressing room mirror. I barely had time to think about anyone or anything from home as I hustled from one class to another on the unfamiliar campus and took notes on poems I had never read. Nightly international phone calls were out of the question—too expensive—so I went out and drank dark, chewy beer and met Italian boys who introduced themselves by asking, "Are you Swedish?" It became a joke among my friends that wherever we went, someone would walk up and ask me that question (it was my blond hair, we figured). It got to the point where I thought, hell, I *could* be Swedish. I could be anybody over here. I could, most certainly, be a girl who doesn't spend all her time working on her relationship with a poison man.

When you make poor choices (and when you've watched a good deal of TV in your day), you start to feel like you're living a movie about a person who makes poor choices. Your props and scenery conform to your narrative and become complicit in keeping you in it: The stop sign at the end of your street that you pass every time you drive to see him. Your mailbox. The dresses in your closet. The Rice Krispies in your bowl, crackling their witness. All these things right there in front of you every day cue you to show up as that person, that character, you've been. It's hard to believe you could be anyone else.

This is why you have to change your scenery.

It's why, for example, you have to move out of your child-hood room at some point. It's why you have to trade your old T-shirt for a blouse. It's why you have to ditch your flip-flops and get a pair of shoes with soles when you're going to interview for a job. It's never really about the room or the blouse or the shoes. It's about you and which story you're living.

In my strange new surroundings at Cambridge, not a single stop sign or traffic light or cereal box signaled me to pick up where I had left off back home. My new room looked nothing like my old room. It had different carpet, different furniture, a different closet (with a sink in it!)—and no phone, which meant no answering machine. And so I broke the cycle of checking voice mail every time I came home, heart pounding in anticipation of an angry message from him or, worse, no message at all. I stopped mentally rehashing our past conver-sations, a habit I'd developed when trying to figure out what I'd done wrong to make him let me down in whatever latest way he had. My head was full of new conversations now, with voices in new accents. I discovered a new favorite food—the Brie-salad sandwich—and as I sat eating with friends on a bridge overlooking the River Cam one sunny afternoon, I realized that I no longer thought of my poisonous relationship in the present tense. I thought of it as a memory, a story that had happened to a person who was *then-me* but not *now-me*. Mostly I thought, *Damn, I'm so glad that's over.*

It was as if I'd finally harnessed the power of all those moves I'd made as a child. Moving had always put my old world behind me, which seemed unfair when I was a kid and didn't want to leave the world I was in, but now? To be able to remove myself from one story and put myself somewhere new—to drink and watch and wear new things until my new setting became familiar enough to support a whole new character, a new me? What a miracle. What a relief.

One evening on my way into town for a night out, I ducked away from my friends into a phone booth. I got out my emergency prepaid phone card and made the call. I told him I didn't miss him anymore, I wouldn't be seeing him again, it was over.

"We'll work on things when you get home," he replied.

"No," I said. "No more working on it."

As I hung up the receiver, I felt the conversation disappear down the wires into a tiny fizzling flicker of nothing. *The end.* Last scene. Roll credits.

# Good Job

**A** friend of mine recently got a Roomba—one of those auto-mated robot vacuums that cleans your house. We sat at her kitchen counter and watched it navigate the floor. It motored along in one direction, then hit a wall or the leg of a chair, spun around, and headed the other way. It zigged and zagged across the rug, bouncing off obstacles—eager and blind, purposeful and aimless at the same time.

"Look," my friend said. "It's like a drunk bee."

"Or us in our twenties," I said.

"Entropy = disorder. Time progresses, entropy in the universe increases, things fall apart." I wrote this on page one of my notebook in my first chemistry class at Davidson, which I took because I was sure I would be heading to medical school after college. Is there any creature more confident in her future plans than a college freshman who has yet to complete a single semester?

There were more doctors in my family than any other professionals, and I understood what the physician's path looked like—med school, residency, practice. It took that chemistry class plus a year of calculus to make me realize that wailing and gnashing teeth over molecular diagrams and indecipherable equations was not a behavior I should indulge in for several more years of schooling, and that I might not have been cut out for the mathematical aspects of life in the medical field.

English, on the other hand? Joy! Three hours writing a paper beats three hours measuring the levels of corrosive liquid in a test tube any day. I declared my major and made it my goal to graduate with high honors. Bang—done. But then?

I knew I loved to write, but to me, "writer" meant novelist, which I'd never wanted to be, or journalist, which didn't appeal to me, what with so much boring fact-checking. As a little kid, I used to sit at breakfast, reading the back of the Cheerios box and editing it in my head to make it snappier and more interesting ("crunchy Os"—really? How 'bout "tiny whole-grain life preservers"?), yet it never occurred to me that someone *did* that as a profession.

I saw no point in going to grad school for English, because the goal of that path seemed to be a job as an English professor, and if there's one thing I cannot do at all (other than maintain balance while walking down stairs in high heels or self-administer a bikini wax), it's teach. I was once invited to guest-teach a poetry class for a day in college, during which hour I shot rapid-fire questions at the class while growing increasingly peeved at their slow response time, until one kid finally yelled, "Could you GIVE US A MINUTE?" Afterward I ducked into a stairwell and rage-cried. So, no—not teaching. Process of elimination didn't leave me with much.

Mostly, as my friends seemed to plug along in pursuit of their postgraduation dreams, I stared terrified into the abyss, wondering if I'd be able to see my dream once my eyes adjusted to the darkness. Looking back, I realize pretty much everyone felt as lost as I did. But I didn't know that then, and I wanted a plan of my own. I would not allow entropy.

The easiest thing for a diligent student to do is to accept an assignment. So the summer between my junior and senior years of college, I tricked the professional world into solving the problem for me by playing internship roulette. That is, rather than apply for jobs in a field in which I wanted to work, I applied to a program that matched up interns with openings. I couldn't answer the question "What do you want to do?"—so I asked, "Well, what do *you* think I should do?" Show me what to want, and I'll show you how I can get it.

I ended up being placed with an organization called Arts and Citizens, the mission of which was to raise awareness and funds for the humanities. I didn't have the first clue as to what I would be doing, but I very much liked that out of all the applicants in the program, an employer had picked me. Plus, I knew what "arts" were, and I knew what "citizens" were, even if I didn't really know how one might "raise awareness and funds."

I learned a lot as an arts advocate. I learned, for example, that there are some questions you should ask in the course of the interview process. Specifically, ask the agency if all the organizations participating in the program know that they signed up for it and are actually expecting an intern to show up. You may be surprised to find that the answer is no. I don't think my boss remembered applying for an intern, or at least didn't expect that she'd really be granted one. She was a polite, quiet, Patagonia-fleece-wearing gal of about forty, always clutching a sheaf of ripped-open envelopes as if she'd started opening the mail and forgotten to finish, and she looked up at me in surprise every morning when I walked through her door. She was the only other person I ever saw in this internship, because—here's another thing I learned—sometimes the term *organization* is used loosely to describe a one-person letter-writing effort that operates out of a storage room above a theater. The "organization" might be just one desk and one chair for that one person, a set of supply shelves containing various paper products, and an enormous, ancient computer with a black screen and a blinking green cursor and a keyboard that goes KABOING every time you hit a key. (Time to write a form letter: KABOING KABOING. KABOING KABOING KABOING.)

I learned that after an intern has organized the office supplies, mailed the letters, made the pot of tea, and procured the sandwiches for lunch for both herself and the boss, there is a lot of workday left. Not capable of simply doing nothing for the afternoon, I applied myself very industriously to looking industrious. I stacked the Post-its by size, by color, and by shape. I walked to the post office and checked the mail twice a day. I often felt nervous, my work-engine idling uncomfortably.

Things got better after I found another, smaller storage

closet in the theater attic and commandeered it as my office. I took yellow legal pads in there with me and came out periodically to announce that I had made a list of all the supplies that were running low (down one legal pad since yesterday!).

"Would it be helpful for me to make a trip to Office Depot?" I'd ask.

"No, we're fine," my boss would say, and I'd go back to sorting pens.

Had I not received a check at the end of the summer, I'm not sure I could prove the internship really even happened.

The biggest thing I learned from wandering out into the workforce, flipping on my "available" light, and letting myself be grabbed by the first open hand that came along was this: It feels good to be chosen for something, but making a life requires making some choices yourself, too. At the very least, one ought to know what one is applying to be chosen *for*. I'd been so paralyzed by the prospect of deciding what to do for a summer—because what if this one job was the beginning of what I'd do for the rest of my whole life?—that I couldn't even pick a direction. As a result, I ended up sitting in a closet for two months.

A few months after that internship and a decade and a half after I crushed my fellow first graders at spelling, I turned that childhood victory into my law school application essay. I wrote five hundred words on how exceeding expectations helps you (that is, me) win at life. Did I get into law school? Yes, I did. Did I go to law school? No, I did not. But I applied because that was what liberal arts majors without any clear career path did, and I desperately wanted a path. I needed to know that once school ended, I'd still have goals to reach for—if not grades to earn, then professional accomplishments to rack up. I wanted a ladder with rungs, a hierarchy with titles, some structure to place around my need to achieve. I was afraid to exist without succeeding; I just had to figure out what to succeed at.

It was only when the acceptance letters started rolling in that I realized what I had done. One Saturday afternoon in February of my senior year, I sat on my little plank of a dorm room bed and looked at the letters spread out on my lap, my dog-eared LSAT prep book lying on the floor under a pile of spiral notebooks and binders. I pictured three years in law school—taking tests, writing papers. That, I could imagine. I loved school. But when I envisioned my life after those three years were over—late nights scouring tiny print for loopholes, long days yelling about things in court like on *Law & Order*—I felt nothing. What an idiot. I'd been so shortsighted that I'd chased the nearest A+ all the way into a corner.

*Shit*, I thought.

Graduation was coming, and if I wasn't going to law school, I had no plan at all.

One company was still holding recruiting meetings with students on campus. I signed up at the careers office, pulled off a great act of bullshitting magic in the interview, and convinced the recruiter from Accenture that despite my abject lack of tech experience, I was totally suited to a job as a software consultant. When I got the job offer, I told myself it was the same as grad school admittance, because it meant I had succeeded, I was *chosen*. I wrote letters back to the law schools: *With gratitude and apologies, I must decline. . . .*

As a fresh college graduate and new analyst in a consulting firm in Charlotte, North Carolina, I had to follow a prescribed set of steps: (1) Go off to training camp and learn how to code software (ha HAAAA haaaaaa, WHAT?), and (2) be dispatched with a team of more experienced consultants to a company that needs some kind of software system to improve their business. My first assignment after training was at a major bank. Let's call it SuperBank.

Here's what I loved about my first year on the job: the outfits. The navy suit that also looked good if you put the navy jacket over gray pants, and the tweed shift that worked with either a black cardigan or the gray jacket that came with the gray pants, and the chocolate-brown skirt that went great with everything. I owned three pairs of low-heeled pumps: navy, black, and brown faux crocodile ("mock croc," if you will, and I did). The fact that all of these things coordinated, making them practically mistake-proof when it came to mixing-and-matching, did not prevent me from wearing one black shoe and one navy shoe to work more than once. I painted my nails neutral colors to go with my professional ensembles: clear, slightly less clear, or pale pink. One time I got crazy and did metallic beige, but I felt self-conscious about it after six hours and took it off.

It was the dawn of Dilbert. The age of cubicle culture.

There was a popular book out at the time called *Who Moved My Cheese?* I read it, because I read every how-to-be-a-businessperson book I could get my hands on, but I couldn't tell you today what it was about. I think there was an analogy wherein business people were mice in a maze. And the cheese was whatever they were looking for . . . money? Opportunity? The feeling of achieving something that proved you were worth the oxygen you breathed? (Maybe that was just me.)

Our project group—a mix of consultants from my company and financial specialists from SuperBank—occupied the thirty-seventh floor of the SuperBank office tower. Nose-high cubicle walls divided the floor into modular quadrants. I had to memorize people's cube decorations to find my way to and from the elevators. There was Stephanie's red college pennant; there was Derek's little bendy horse he'd gotten as a Happy Meal prize because we were all in our early twenties and still often ate like children; there was the clip-on fan Adam had rigged up over his desk; turn left; there was my cube. The size of your cube indicated your station in this professional society: tiny for an analyst; less tiny for a consultant; even less tiny for a manager, plus a small extra chair for cubicle guests.

Our team was charged with testing the software that would go into all the new SuperBank ATM machines. Kicking the technological tires, so to speak. The elder consultants explained to us newbies what software testing entailed: writing scripts for scenarios wherein you imagine how a person might use the software—in our case, scripts for how a person would use an ATM machine. Then another team would use those scripts to test the ATMs, making sure everything worked, and fixing what didn't.

I couldn't even think of more than maybe four scenarios for what could happen at an ATM. Get money. Don't get money. Check your balance. Deposit a check? What else was there? I tried very hard to write good scripts—I asked my coworkers to sit down and show me, time and again, how to come up with different plots for this ATM story—but I flailed helplessly when I got back to my cube. I'd stare at the phone on my desk, willing it to light up with a call from someone a few cubes away wanting to take a break and get coffee. I loved coffee breaks, but even with enough breaks to sip more caffeine than it could possibly have been healthy to consume, every workday felt sixty hours long.

I loved my coworkers, but I hated my job. Putting together outfits wasn't enough, and often, when I got back to my little apartment each night to boil my pasta and watch *Ally McBeal*, I wondered, *How much longer can I fake this?* I suspected not much longer, but I couldn't imagine the next page in my own script either.


I stuck with the consulting company for a few years, transferring from Charlotte to the Atlanta office when John and I got married, but I never did feel like I fit in, which is why I developed a lunchtime habit of scrolling through online job postings. I was looking at jobs over a bowl of soup one day when I saw a listing for a copywriter. Copywriter? That's a thing? Like, a writer, but not novels or journalism? Perfect! I looked it up, and sure enough, this was a real job you could get paid for. A local hospital was looking for a writer to join their in-house communications team, to craft ads making their hospital sound better than other hospitals, write brochures about various diseases, and report heartstring-yanking stories about sick children to use in fundraising campaigns. I drafted a cover letter explaining why this job was my true calling ("Having grown up in a medical household but majoring in English . . .") and attached copies of emails I'd written at Accenture as writing samples. They hired me. I took a big pay cut, and an even bigger leap of faith, when I accepted the job.

As soon as I finished filling out my new-employee paperwork and had a moment of quiet in my tiny new office at the hospital, I opened up my box of business cards. I marveled at the title under my name: *Writer*.

Had I done it? Was this my destiny? Could Cheerios boxes be far away? Other questions bubbled in the back of my mind. If I were taking a class called "Career," would this change be considered a bad grade because my salary went backward? Or a good grade, because I was doing something more aligned with my real interests? I couldn't be sure, so I decided to grade this choice on courage and gave myself an A for bravery.

This job is where my writing career began, and it firmly fits into the category of *paying one's dues*. I learned to manage an editorial calendar, to write fast on demand, and to stick to word limits. I also learned to tolerate an erratic editor prone to striking red slashes across whole pages, to throw away and rewrite copy again and again after the scope or messaging got changed by someone else, and to meet deadlines that mysteriously bounced around the calendar. (I also learned to avoid being alone in the break room with a male colleague who once looked at my wrap blouse and asked, "If I pull that string, will your shirt come off?") I believe every working writer needs a starter job like this. Minus the asshole.

Unfortunately, our departmental budget got cut after I'd been there about a year, and after that our boss's boss left and the resulting backlogs made productivity a joke. People started quitting and not being replaced. Overwork led to disorganization. Chaos.

I developed a rash on my neck, and my dermatologist asked, "Are you often around sources of irritation?" Yes, I was.

I knew I had to leave, but I was disappointed to have to change jobs again. I wanted to get somewhere and *stay*. I wanted to run right up to some final prize and touch it and hear a *ding!* for done. I just didn't know what the prize was.

When I joined the national home office of the American Cancer Society in Atlanta, I thought, *This is it. Finally.* In my role there, I wrote the first company-wide editorial style guide, which meant I got to tell people, *We use apostrophes like this, not like that. These are the rules.* I wrote speeches about the fight against cancer that were then spoken from the mouths of CEOs and celebrities. I met President George H. W. Bush when he received a medal of honor for his work promoting research. I worked on ad campaigns that played on the radio and aired on TV and won awards. (Awards!)

Three days after September 11, 2001, my boss asked me to accompany our chief operating officer across the street to the Centers for Disease Control and Prevention headquarters, where they needed to create a crisis communications plan to use in the event of biological terrorism.

"Why me?" I asked. I didn't even work for the CDC—they were just our neighbors.

"They need someone who can understand what they're saying and write fast, and I told them you could do it," he said.

Me! They needed me. Because I was good at what I did. Something breathtakingly terrible had happened in the world and everyone felt helpless, but I could do a tiny thing to help. That felt like success, for a few days anyway.


As the "war on terror" raged, the world spun into a state of heightened unrest. The longer we lived, it seemed, the more terribly human beings treated each other. The nightly news became more frightening, not less. The planet suffered more, not less. And I felt more aimless at work, not less. The hits of success at my ACS job were regular and sweet, so why, when I got home at the end of the day, did I often feel as adrift as I did after a day at SuperBank? I waited for a sense of completion, the peace I expected from a job well done, but it didn't come.

What did I think would happen? That I'd do the job for a

few years and then they'd say, *Well, cancer is over, you solved it.* And then I'd do every other job in the world to finality, and every company on earth would eventually close because I finished everything? Step forward to accept your prize and be turned into a rainbow—the work of the universe is over!

For the first time in my life, I began to realize that I couldn't reach that prize I was searching for, because there was no such prize. Not in these jobs, or in any job. I could plug away toward triumph and fulfillment, which shimmered on the road ahead, always so close, but no accomplishment would ever be the A+ I needed to feel I'd done enough. The best I could hope for was to make some small dent of impact on the ever-increasing mess of our world and to enjoy it for the fleeting moment it lasted.

What I'd learned about entropy came back to me: *We are always moving deeper into chaos.* That thought lodged in my soul and got stuck. *What if this is it?* I often thought. *What if work is just a thing we do to distract ourselves from the fact that the world is falling apart?* In that case, it doesn't even matter what job you do or how well you do it. Why do any of us clock in and out every day? Is this why people take early retirement from their accounting firms and go work as fishing guides?


A month before I left to have my first child, I told my supervisors at ACS I wouldn't be coming back. *Take your maternity leave and get paid*, they said. *You might change your mind.* I said no, I couldn't take money from a nonprofit for a job I didn't intend to return to. I wanted to be with my baby for a while, to figure out what parenthood was like and consider the future. I would always work in some capacity, I knew, but I needed to think about how. I needed to think about this:

All this time, I'd wanted to do a job so well that I'd feel *done*. I wanted to accomplish enough to *be* good enough. But if that wasn't possible, then the very condition I'd been working so hard to avoid—being uncertain and unfinished—might be unavoidable. It might just be how life was, and everyone else had known it all along, like they all knew what a lobsterman was, and I'd been working my ass off like a mouse on a wheel, not realizing that I was running toward cheese that wasn't even there.

# This Guy

**Hootie** and the Blowfish played a concert in our college gymnasium. (Hellooooo, 1990s.) It was the last campus show they did before hitting the big time; the next night, they were on *David Letterman*. As they launched into the opening notes of their breakout hit, "Hold My Hand," some inebriated boy off to the side of the speakers threw his hands into the air. "HOLD MY HAND!" he yelled. "HOLLLD MYYYYYY HAAAAAAAND!"

*Who is that drunken fool?* I wondered.

Ladies and gentlemen, that drunken fool is now the father of my children.

(For the record, he is not regularly drunken or foolish.)

If you met him, you would want to marry him. But you can't, because I already did. You know how people say, "You just know," and you roll your eyes and make that gagging motion with your finger in your mouth? Well, I just knew. We officially met my junior year, his senior year, a week or so post-Hootie. He walked over to my group of girlfriends where we were leaning up against a fence watching a soccer game and asked us, "So what are you all doing tonight?" We had plans to go to an off-campus house for a guy's birthday party, so I said, "We're going to Dan's."

"You're going to dance?" He started dancing, waving his arms around in an approximation of a hula. Then he took my hand, lifted it over my head, and twirled me.

On one of our early dates, we were curled up on the sofa in his apartment watching a movie. I was in agonizing pain from monthly cramps. I didn't want to make a big deal of it—nothing fans those sexy flames like period talk—but it had reached a truly distracting level of misery. Eventually I had to fess up as to why I couldn't get comfortable. "You probably just need some naproxen," he said. "I'll go get some." He paused the movie, put a blanket over my legs, and drove off to the pharmacy. When, upon his return, I marveled at his behavior, he explained that he'd grown up with a twin sister. "Girl stuff," as he said, didn't faze him.

Later, I overheard him on the phone with his sister, whom he'd called for no reason other than that he loved her and wanted to check in. He did this with his parents, too. His side of the calls with them was all "Yes, ma'am" and "Yes, sir" and "What can I do for you?" His Southern manners reminded me of my grandparents, and I loved how sweet he was, how naturally loving.

He proposed a couple of years later, after we'd graduated, when he was twenty-three and I was twenty-one. If you're twenty-three or twenty-one and you tell me you've just gotten engaged, I will tell you that you're insane and too young, because when I look at twenty-one- and twenty-three-year-olds now, they look like babies. But at the time, when I was twenty-one, I could not foresee any reason not to marry him. I pictured the timeline of my life ahead of me—inasmuch as a twenty-one-year-old can look at her future life, which is to say in hazy, imaginary terms—and saw no circumstance in which I'd want *not* to be married to him. Would I want not to be married in fifty years because we'd grow sick of each other? Would I want not to be married after we'd had kids and parenthood changed us? Would I want not to be married if we didn't have kids? No, no, no. I would never want not to be married to him. I was sure.

Plus, come on, could there be someone better out there for me to find? No, again. And as preposterous as my confidence was on every other question, on this one I was right. I found the best person early. I got lucky.

Marrying John was not an attempt to get an A+ in relationships. It was both the rightest thing I've ever done and the thing that had the least to do with the question of "What is right?" This sounds like I'm giving cheesy advice, saying the right way to find love is to stop thinking and follow your heart. That's not it. I mean, row your love-canoe down the river of dreams or whatever, but what I'm trying to say is that the evolution of a relationship is not something you can entirely control. Falling in love is not a matter of weighing pros and cons. Unlike other big life events—jobs, moves, homes—it's not a thing you work toward like you're seeking a personal-life promotion. You don't pick a human being and go, okay, now we're going to follow these steps and fall in love and reach the certain knowledge that we want to be together forever. I don't care what the secret-to-love books and articles say, that's not how it works. It wasn't for us, anyway. We met. It happened.

The spontaneous existence of love where before there was none is the most insanely wondrous thing. It's crazy magic. You might as well witness your hairbrush transforming into a talking owl right before your eyes.

We do disagree sometimes. But often when we fight, it's not really fighting at all. It usually goes like this:

I, deeply unsettled by some existential horror but not willing to face and discuss the existential horror, pick a fight about something else. Often, I take this opportunity after John has benignly pointed out something I'm doing wrong. For example: I decide to reheat some leftovers in a Styrofoam container. As I put it in the oven, John says, "Hey, Styrofoam melts. Shouldn't you put that food in a pan?"

I say something sarcastic to indicate I couldn't possibly be wrong. ("Why would a restaurant put leftovers in a container that can't be reheated? I know how an oven works.")

John presents evidence to support his point, thinking he's helping. ("Uh-oh, look—the Styrofoam is dissolving.")

I lash out at John and accuse him of calling me stupid. ("WELL, THIS IS OBVIOUSLY SOME FAULTY STYROFOAM. AND MAYBE YOU COULD COOL IT WITH THE GLOATING.")

John says he is not calling me stupid, and offers to help

correct whatever is happening because of the thing I have done wrong. ("Okay, I'm just going to put out the fire in the oven.")

I stomp off in a snit.

Fifteen minutes later, I come back and tell him whatever's really bothering me. ("I'm sad that summer is almost over and seasons keep changing and the kids are getting big and soon they'll leave us and I'll miss them so much I'll die.")

John listens. I talk more. I flap my hands around in wild gestures; he watches. I exhale in a big huff, and he exhales, too, to match me.

Fifteen minutes after that, I'm in good spirits again.


When I am packing a suitcase and I've crammed every last rectangle of folded clothing into the bag and added shoes, makeup, a just-in-case-it's-cold cardigan and a panicked last-minute backup outfit or two, and I'm mashing everything down as hard as I can, and I go from zero to psycho in a second because I can't get the bag zipped, and I'm stomping on the bag and hammering at it with my fists, he calmly opens it, rearranges a few things, and zips it.

Sometimes he says exactly what pops into his head. On a visit to Augusta: Over dinner, my mother picked up some fancy little utensil—a silver fish knife or something—and held it up. "That's pretty," John said, dutifully offering a compliment. "Well, it'll be yours one day," my mom said. "When you're dead?" John responded. He heard his words as they came out and immediately reddened, throwing his hands over his mouth. "Yes, when I'm dead," she answered, as the rest of us laughed.

We went to celebrate our daughter's birthday in her kindergarten classroom, where there was a tradition of letting the children climb up on the tables and have a dance party. The teachers put something innocuous on the speakers—"The Wheels on the Bus," maybe. But before the music started, we looked over to see our girl, hands thrown over her head, doing a body roll and singing, "THIS GIRL IS ON FIIIIRE." The teacher looked aghast. I looked aghast. John looked from the teacher to me, and, sensing my embarrassment, blurted, "I taught her that." (He didn't teach her that. I taught her that. We often danced in the kitchen at home.)

He is the dad who, when I feel myself losing my mind at the repetitive nature of homework—it's spelling words on the green sofa all over again!—will take the stack of flash cards and the third grader and go out to the porch and tackle the addition tables until they are finished. He can supervise the cleaning of rooms without losing his patience. He can teach them how to ride a bike without trying to micromanage their every turn.

He is the person you call when you find a living or dead animal where it shouldn't be, and he calmly wields the net or the shovel. I make the grocery list with the items listed in the order in which they occur as one walks from left to right through the store aisles; he goes and does the shopping. I point out the spiderwebs in the windows; he takes a broom and whisks them away. I see one dead plant and freak out about global warming; he turns on the hose and waters it. He doesn't get flustered, grossed out, or panicked. Where I see things in disarray and feel overwhelmed at how much in the world there is to fix, he picks up a hammer or pen or trash bag and starts chipping away at it. When I'm a planet come loose from its orbit, trying to find its place while bouncing around space like a pinball, this guy is the sun itself. This is how we operate.

He is the most important person in my life. Well, now one of the three most important people, although it started with just him. But he is not my "other half." Our lives move forward as a unit and also as the lives of two individuals. We are not a couple who share one email address. (That's weird. Sorry, "JanAndGaryFleming@gmail.com.") We were each a person before, and we are each a person still.

A marriage does not make anybody more of a real person or a right person. It makes you a married person. You can be a wonderful married person or a terrible married person, just like you can be a wonderful not-married person or a terrible not-married person. You can also be a wonderful person who has a dog or a terrible person who has a dog, a wonderful or terrible person who has no dog, a wonderful or terrible person who has a baby or does not.

So, marrying John did not make me a good person, or a successful person. But it did make me very happy.

And when I look back on my twenties, a decade during which I was bullheadedly focused on checking all the boxes in order to be a good adult, I can see what a blessing it was to have some things in my life that weren't tied to success or failure, especially the love of a person whom I often joked was exactly what I would have created for myself had I been wise enough to know what I really needed—but who was 100 percent not of my own making. I could take no credit for working this love into existence, and that made it a respite, both at the time and many years later.

# Welcome to the Club

**When** I blew out the candle on my twenty-fifth birthday cupcake at the kitchen counter of our tiny new house, I wished for a leaf blower. So I went to Ace Hardware the following weekend and bought one—a reasonably priced and sized model with a tiny gas tank (so I wouldn't have to drag an electrical cord around) and a small motor (because the superpowered ones came with backpacks that, when I tried them on, tipped me over backward). I flaunted my leaf blower in the yard of that house, a brick shoebox surrounded by a square plot of grass and four tremendous oak trees, which for nine months out of the year rained skinny brown leaves upon the ground, creating a thick, slippery layer that slid out from under your feet as you walked and made car tires spin on the short, precipitously steep driveway. I hoped the neighbors would see me blasting leaves around: Behold, I do yard things, just like you.

I wanted to prove my membership in their club, a neighborhood populated by couples a decade or more older than John and me, most with school-age children. They had to have looked at us—this silly little couple in our mid-twenties—and thought, *Babies*. I looked at us and thought, *Grown-ups*. We were married, after all. Married people have homes. And leaf blowers! This is what you do. This is stability.

I knew my yard-care efforts had been successful at establishing our adult credentials when we received a card in the mailbox, our first invitation to the neighborhood supper club:

DINNER CLUB

SATURDAY, 7 P.M.

DISCO INFERNO

Disco motherfucking inferno. YES. Not even five years out of college, we still knew how to do it up for a theme party. In fact, we still had theme party costumes in our closets. I dug up the groovetaculous polyester dress I'd worn to a '70s party senior year. Floor length, aqua with orange and green stripes, spaghetti straps. *Glorious*. John wore a fly thrift-shop ensemble, including an enormous pair of sunglasses and a paisley shirt made of some flammable man-made material—unbuttoned to his navel, natch.

We set out for the party on foot, making our way around the corner to the hosts' house.

"Do we know anyone's names?" John asked as I rang the doorbell.

"They're going to love us," I said. This would be the night the neighbors went from including us to embracing us, I was sure. It might even be the night they held a spontaneous election and named me president of the supper/leaf blower/adult club.

A man answered the door. He stared. "You must be the new neighbors."

We looked at him, in his khakis and loafers, then looked

past him to the living room, where everyone was in sweater sets and button-down shirts.

Turns out nobody ever dressed up for supper club. The "theme" applied to the food and decor, not the attire.

I might have been aware of this had I taken the time to get to know our neighbors a little bit before waltzing into their lives in a rainbow prom gown.

Whenever you join a group of some sort, there's an orientation period where you need to learn the lingo, observe the customs of the tribe, and gauge where everyone stands in the social pecking order. You're provisional members, so to speak. You've got to hang around long enough for people to get used to you. You can't just assume that because you've reached a particular level in the game of life, you immediately fit in with those who have been there much longer. Unless you're me, in which case you point at the house and go, "I AM ONE OF YOU NOW. I BLOW LEAVES."

Having a home, I figured, means you belong. I belonged in a house made of bricks (because I read "The Three Little Pigs" and learned from it), a 1940s bungalow in the center of Atlanta. Our neighborhood was bordered by a creek on one side and a highway on the other. A historical marker sign indicated the site of a Civil War battle. We'd bought into something established. I was going to excel at homeownership.

That's why, after we got a leaf blower and figured out the rules of supper club, we got a dog, followed shortly by another dog. Because two dogs is not just an accidental dog; it's intentional dog ownership, and everyone knows you have to have dogs before you have babies, because being great at owning a dog is how you show the world you're ready for children. Obviously.

Our dogs, two beagles named Frances and Phoebe, owned the following:

- One hairbrush, shared
- One sweater each
- Collar tags engraved with name, address, phone number, and rabies vaccination license number
- A large beanbag bed
- Developmentally appropriate toys, such as rubber domes with little holes in them that shook out treats at random intervals, thus stimulating the dogs' natural foraging instincts and keeping their minds sharp, because who wants a dull-minded hound?

I interviewed several dog walkers before hiring Angela, a career walker who came with strong references and a well-articulated philosophy regarding canine individuality. She came to our house twice a day while John and I were at work and spent twenty minutes with the dogs each time. As per our agreement, she left page-long narratives about the day's activities on a notepad near the front door. "We watched the trash truck today. Frances is getting faster at chasing squirrels. Two Milk-Bones at 3 o'clock. Phoebe likes the green ones best."

The beauty of having a real house, not an apartment, is that you can just open the back door and let the dogs out, which I did every morning at 5:45 a.m., when John's alarm went off and he got in the shower and I made my coffee. Such a well-oiled machine, this household.

We'd been in the house maybe two months when our neighbors called.

"Your dogs are waking up our kids," the woman said.

"My dogs don't know your kids," I replied.

"Our bedrooms are right across the fence from your backyard," she said. "Every time your dogs bark to come in, they wake us up."

*How rude*, I thought. We didn't know much about these neighbors yet other than that both the man and woman worked long hours, and their daughter and son looked to be . . . two-ish? Three? I had no sense of children's ages. They weren't babies, but they couldn't drive. So whatever age that is. And apparently their parents didn't like us.

"Those people hate dogs," I told John.

"Maybe they don't hate dogs. Maybe they just like their sleep," he said.

"They're so mean."

Having thrown down what I saw as a completely irrational gauntlet, the neighbors made their disdain clearer by never complimenting me on my neat rows of leaf bags or my seasonal plantings in the pots by our front door. I couldn't believe how unfriendly they were. And I couldn't believe the woman kept calling me.

"It's just that when I finally get them down to sleep, I really need them to stay asleep," she said. "Could you maybe try letting the dogs in and out a different door?"

This was rich, I thought. She was trying to tell me which doors to use in my own house, when we both knew that their giant white cat had been prancing along the fence between our yards and taunting Frances and Phoebe, which was probably why they were barking.

"Maybe if you kept your cat in your yard, my dogs wouldn't bark so much," I suggested.

It was a classic border war. Cats versus dogs. Neighbor versus neighbor. As months passed, we developed a chilly stalemate in which they kept asking us to please quiet our dogs and we (okay, I) kept telling them to keep their cat to themselves, but nothing really changed.

The way I figured it, we were both homeowners with pets, and one household—the one that was not ours—was being awfully bossy toward the other one. I did not think about how I'd feel if somebody's dogs were waking up my babies every time I put them to sleep. I had no babies; I didn't get it. I didn't comprehend how different my neighbor's life was from mine, how much more she had to balance, how much more precious and rare her full nights of rest were.

When I'm being hard on myself, I call myself a bitch for how insensitive I was. When I'm being more understanding, I remind myself that no one can fully appreciate a life phase or experience they haven't lived through. Someone might explain to you what it feels like, and even though you understand the words—they are all nouns and verbs you know; you know what a *baby* is, you know what *sleep* is—you don't *understand*. You have empathy and intelligence, but empathy and intelligence have limits. So many arguments come down to saying, "Of course I understand what you mean," while not understanding what the other person really means at all, because you can't. Today-me tries to cut back-then-me a little slack.

What I did know was that neither the cat nor the dogs were any good at keeping rats away. North Georgia wood rats are terrier-size, and they specialize in climbing trees and then jumping onto your house and eating a hole in your roof and going into your attic and then busting through your closet ceiling and having babies in the pockets of your winter coats.

We also had a mold problem, which we didn't notice until the mold had crept silently up from the crawl space, through the wood floors, across the living room rug and up the side of a sofa. I can only guess that rats love mold, because both things lived very happily in our home alongside us without our knowledge for quite some time. Coincidentally, both required expensive extermination services.

I was looking over the bill from the mold remediation company and questioning whether homeownership was worth it one rainy Sunday afternoon when the neighbor called.

"Have you seen our cat?" he asked. "He's been missing since yesterday."

"Oh no," I said. I didn't like the dog-taunting little feline creep, but I didn't want anything bad to happen to him. I'd always been an animal lover, and the thought of the cat having encountered some danger softened me a bit toward our neighbors for a moment.

"Could I come check your crawl space?" he asked.

"Oh, there's no way he could be in there," I explained. "It's bolted shut. No one can get into it without removing the door with a screwdriver."

"Can I just look?"

Holy *Dateline* special, our neighbors thought we'd buried their cat alive. My heart hardened right back up.

"Fine," I said.

John went out in the rain with his tools, and our neighbor held an umbrella over the bushes that obscured the two-foot-square wooden door that led into the dark underbelly of our house, a dank tunnel where the pipes snaked under our floors.

When he pulled the door away from the house, out bolted the big white ghost cat.

John stepped back onto a slick of oak leaves, knocking over a tightly packed leaf bag, which exploded like a bomb, shooting leaves into the air.

We never figured out how that cat got in there, although we suspect he wandered in after a rat while the mold guy had the door off the crawl space the day before.

We did, however, eventually figure out why barking dogs are so upsetting to parents of young children. We looked back, after some years, and saw the gulf between where we were and where our neighbors were and how little we knew. I never apologized, but in the years that followed the births of our own babies, I spoke to our neighbors in the contrite tones of a person who is ashamed to admit, but knows without question, that she was wrong.

# The Window

**"Should** I have kids?"

Several times over the past few years, I've been invited to lunch by younger friends who eventually push the chips and guacamole aside and get down to asking this question. I remember asking it—or a version of it—of a friend of mine years ago. I was twenty-five and she was thirty-two, and she'd just announced her pregnancy. "Why?" I asked (which, just so you know, is considered a strange response to a pregnancy announcement). I meant, "How did you know it was time?" and "What made you sure you wanted to?" and "Did you always know this would happen?" I wanted her to tell me something about my own future.

I'm now a woman in my forties and I have children, so maybe it looks like I have knowledge and perspective on this matter. But I know only my own experience, and if there's one question that doesn't have a one-size-fits-all answer, it's this one. No one is really qualified to give anyone else an answer, although that doesn't stop anybody from asking.

---

Here's what I usually say: Have kids! You're going to be great! I love my kids so much, I think my head will explode!

And if the other person starts to look terrified, I say: Don't have them! That's cool! You'll have such a good life! Think of all you'll do with your time and resources!

And if they sit through either of those answers and keep looking me in the eyes, waiting me out, I say: Okay, you want to know the truth? Having children made me wish for a time machine.

I explain it like so:

I knew I wanted kids, and I knew I wanted to be a young mother—partly because my parents had me in their twenties and that seemed like as good a model to follow as any, and partly because I have this "do the work first, have fun later" mind-set. Having kids seemed like a big job I needed to get started on. Luckily, we married young, so we were able to enjoy some childless married years before we started a family. Then, when we decided it was time, I didn't get pregnant right away . . . or after a year . . . or another year . . . so we ended up jumping through fertility hoops. We were willing to put a lot of time and money and medicine behind the effort, because Mother Nature had worked her baby-wishing spell on us. Every fiber of my being longed to produce a tiny human made of half me, half John.

Our son arrived healthy and gorgeous about ten days before his due date, ushered into daylight via Caesarean section after trying to kick his way out feet-first. In the hospital, cross-eyed on Percocet, I squinted at his little face peeking out of a blanket in my arms. I tried to focus on his impossibly symmetrical eyebrows, a dozen tiny hairs each. When he opened his mouth to cry, tears spilled from the corners of my eyes. "What's wrong?"

John asked. "He's crying," I said, not realizing that I was, too. I wanted to heal my son's pain, soothe his alarm, feed his hunger, do whatever he needed, if I could just figure out what it was. I wanted to do everything right for him.

I knew what brand of car seat to buy and how to wash his blankets in dye-free soap and how to make the temperature of his bathwater match the exact heat of his skin. But there was so much I didn't know. I had never felt such desperate not-knowing.

For instance, I didn't know when I quit my full-time job if that was the right thing to do. I hoped staying home with him would be an A+ move. (Lots of child-rearing books said it was, but then I read an article about "helicopter parenting." Was I doing that already?) Although those early months were everything everyone told me that time would be like—amazing, exhausting, surreal—I felt a little whiplashed, too, having slammed on the productivity brakes so abruptly. At the end of every day, when all I had to show for myself were four peed-on onesies, six diapers, and three and a half hours of sleep, what did those numbers mean? Was I doing a good job? I had a habit of stacking the baby laundry in neat piles on the breakfast table and leaving it there until John got home, just so he'd see some quantifiable proof of my industriousness, like a three-dimensional cotton bar graph. I remember going over to my desk in the kitchen one morning and pulling the abandoned spiral-bound carcass of my work calendar out from under a pile of unopened mail. I found a blank page and scrawled "TAKE SHOWER" in shaky handwriting. Then I showered, put on leggings and a T-shirt, and walked back into the kitchen, wet hair dripping, and crossed it out.

I felt ashamed when I found myself wishing for just an hour of my old life back. Not that I'd give up my baby, not for a second—I just wanted to hit pause, to leave myself and my baby frozen in an embrace with the clock stopped, while I left my present body, inhabited my past self, and visited a life of good sleep and clean clothes and lunch in public and adult conversation. *A time machine*, I thought. *That's all I need.*

I did not know, in those first days, that once you have children, the passage of time feels different than it did before. Everyone says this, and it's true: Days with young children feel four hundred hours long, but years flash by in seconds. I had no idea I'd become one of those parents who posts pictures along with clichéd captions like "And just like that . . . he's ten!" or "Wasn't she a baby just yesterday?" I know, barf. But it *was* just yesterday that my baby boy got so excited about a jar of creamed spinach that he knocked it out of my hands and sent it clattering across his high-chair tray and onto the kitchen floor. I *did* just give birth to my daughter last week. How can they be looking back at me with such grown-up faces right now?

(If you're reading this book in the future, when time machines exist and my children have long since left the nest and moved away, come back and tell me: Did I survive their leaving or did my heart stop?)

I couldn't have predicted or understood how much the start of a baby's life warps an adult's perception of her own childhood.

Suddenly my own spelling bees and birthday parties and child-hood feuds seemed farther in the past than they did before. It was like a dial turned, and—*click*—a new human had appeared at the beginning of the timeline and I was bumped forward a notch into the old-human slot. Yet somehow the opposite felt true as well. When your child is four, you remember things about being four that you hadn't remembered since. My mother got toys out of storage for my son that I had played with, and when I saw them sitting in front of me on the rug, I felt dizzy. If that wooden duck with the paint flecked off its back where little-me once rammed it into a wall can exist right here in front of right-now-me, then surely little-me also still exists and is sitting right here, invisible, with us. It's as if someone put a stitch in time, pulled the thread taut, and yanked a minute from decades ago into the present.

In those moments, it feels as if I actually *do* have a time machine, and it's stuck on a random setting, flinging me back and forth, keeping me present in every stage of life I've experienced. In my mind, I am every person I have ever been. I'm six and the reigning queen of the spelling bee. I'm a teenager, dreaming of a flat in Paris while cursing the flatness of my chest. I'm a terrified new member of the workforce, straight out of college sporting three mix-and-match suits and a briefcase with the tag still on. I'm a freshly stitched-up, squishy mess, home with my infant and drunk on baby love.

Being aware of all these versions of me makes me feel both the presence and absence of all the people I have never been, too. I'm the girl who stayed single and lives in New York and stops at the bodega down the street on my way home every night to get only what I need for my own dinner. I'm a veterinarian. I'm a hermit. I'm Tina Fey and Amy Poehler's third gal pal, and we write movies together on my screened porch. People say friendships don't work in threes, but we prove them all wrong.

These potential selves exist as surely as my past selves do and as truly as the real, right-now self does, too. They happen to live just on the other side of an unseen line—the boundary between past and present, or the border between real and imaginary—but they are *there*.

One of the things I tell nervous young pregnant friends, when they confide that they're freaking out, is not to worry—life happens in phases. You parent a baby, then you parent a toddler, then you parent a kid, and so on. You don't have to know everything about every phase the minute they're born. What I don't say is that this phase thing also sucks. Each phase is all-consuming and then *over*. A time machine would let us slip out of one phase and visit another, live all our lives, be all our selves. A little of this, then a little of that. I can't stand the "or" part of life; I prefer "and." I want to spend a day with my thirteen-year-old daughter and then a day with her as a baby and then a day being a thirteen-year-old myself. I want to be a preschooler again and I want to be a retiree, both for a little while, now.

I don't say that this is the thing I'd ask for if a genie offered me one wish.

Having kids made me think of my parents differently, too. If I'd been bumped out a notch on the timeline, so had they. Not too long ago, I was considering the "your memories from this day" pictures Facebook was showing me from five years earlier and doing that "just yesterday!" thing in my head. Then

I thought: In four sets of five years, I'll be in my sixties. My children will be in their thirties. (How the HELL can that be true?) My parents might be gone. Like a runaway car with no brakes or emergency lever, time was accelerating beyond control. I felt a surge of soul-panic as I held my phone in my hand and looked at that picture: Please *slowdownslowdownslowdown*.

I see my friends caring for their elderly parents, and the role reversal takes my breath away. Moms and dads have turned into old people who have seemingly turned back into toddlers. These once competent adults don't understand how to work things; they refuse to take their medicine; they need help.

It makes me want to hop in the machine and revisit my younger parents. I want to go back to when I was sixteen years old, so I can tell them that although they would not let me stay out past eleven o'clock and I said at the time that they were just mean and didn't want anyone to have fun, I get it now and I'm sorry and they were right. I was never up to any good past that hour, and I should damn well have come home.

I want to go back to even before I was born, to see my mother when she was in college and nicknamed "Wild Mary." Growing up, I found that moniker to be incongruous with the taskmaster who made me take piano lessons on Friday afternoons, although once I graduated from college and got out into the world, she softened considerably. She knitted little round, fuzzy hats for each of my babies, so their little round, fuzzy heads wouldn't get cold. She is still the first person I call when I don't know whether it would be tacky to buy a Christmas wreath made of fake holly or if it's okay to wear a suede jacket in April. I want to go back and tell her then that she will be all of this now.

I want to go back and spend more time with my dad—I haven't called him Daddy in decades, although he still calls me Mary LaLa. I want to listen when he turns up Little Richard songs on the radio to get my mom to dance. I want to make tiny acorn and mushroom cabins again in the greenhouse behind our home in Memphis, where I'd find the butts of his sneaked cigarettes and bury them in the dirt with my tiny garden spade so he wouldn't get caught. I want to be in the kitchen that Thanksgiving in Augusta when he tried to be helpful and wash a pan full of turkey drippings that had been left on the counter, and when my mom saw him squirting Joy dishwashing liquid all over the greasy brown bits, she screamed, "YOU'RE KILLING THE GRAVY WITH JOY," and my brother and I laughed until we couldn't breathe.

I know that one day, I will look to my son—who was my baby five minutes ago, yes, he was—to carry me up the stairs, to drive me to doctor's appointments, to help me when I spill something or can't operate the sleeves of a sweater. He is already taller than me. He will be a man before I can blink. I feel this ahead of me on the timeline and I *need* to get in the time machine and go back. *Please*, I say to the universe. *I can accept all this if you just let me go back sometimes.* Let me nudge the edge of a sippy cup between his lips. Let me comb his matted little fluff of hair. Let me hold his wriggling torso between my knees and button his overalls at his shoulder before he bolts away. If I could just go back and forth. If it weren't all or nothing.

————

I used to want a fancy camera, one with a big, powerful zoom lens. I'd go to the kids' school holiday concerts and try to capture decent shots from the bleachers with my phone, only to wind up with grainy shadowscapes populated with indecipherable little figures. Luckily there was always at least one parent in every class who had a real camera and took perfectly crisp, magazine-worthy photos featuring the unpixelated nostrils and eyelashes of even the back-row xylophone players. Whenever the fancy-camera parents would email everyone else the pictures they took, I'd pull them up on my computer and find myself unable to look away. At first I'd think, yes, I want pictures like this of every moment of childhood. But the more I looked at these exquisite photographs, the more desperate I felt. Such precise visual reminders of exactly what my children looked like in a moment that was irretrievably past thrilled my heart and then broke it. The photo was proof that the split second was over. As sharp as that focus was on their hair, light glimmering on individual strands, that's how sharp the pain was at not being able to reach out my hand and feel its silkiness on my fingers.

It would be better not to be reminded so much—or to be reminded in slightly blurrier terms. I never bought the fancy camera.

In *The Year of Magical Thinking*, Joan Didion wrote that "when we mourn our losses we also mourn, for better or for worse, ourselves. As we were. As we are no longer. As we will one day not be at all." Every despair in the world comes down to this, she believes. Every joy, too, I say. Because every joy will run out. And so will every life. And maybe that's what I mourn as my children grow: the fact that they and I and we will one day not be here at all. No one's getting out of here alive.

If the person I was speaking to is still with me and is looking at me like I'm the voice of doom, I say: Yikes. That got dark fast. Sorry.

I say: Listen, there's so much light on the other side of that darkness, too.

The way a diapered newborn rump fits into a cupped palm? Perfection. The smell of a toddler's clean neck—wondrous. And there may be no greater entertainment than taking a child to the zoo and watching him see a zebra for the first time. A zebra!

A baby's arrival gives us adults the closest thing we'll ever get to magic. There's no person there; then there's a person. You witness the opening of the window between whatever other dimension there is and here. Where did this new soul come from? Who else is over there? It's mind-blowing, because that window must have been there all along, but you're just now noticing it.

That magical time doesn't last, of course. Babies turn into people who walk and talk and eat grilled cheeses, and you think only sometimes—instead of constantly—about how one day they weren't here and then they were and one day they won't be again. Sometimes you don't think about the time machine thing at all.

# Me Real

**When** my daughter was about two and a half, she did something to annoy her brother. I don't remember what—probably committed the heinous crime of tipping over a tower of blocks—but I can still picture how his little cheeks flushed and he clenched his fists as he struggled to express his sudden outrage.

"You!" he sputtered. "You . . . are *temporary*." It was the worst insult he could conjure in the moment, and, to him, a very grown-up one, because it used a newly acquired vocabulary word. (We had recently discussed the difference between a temporary tattoo and a real one. The real one is here to stay; the temporary one isn't.)

Indignant, she bowed up and yelled back, "NO. *Me real!*"

*Poke.*

   *Plunge.*

Every time I jabbed a needle into my belly to inject myself with fertility drugs, I felt like the injection should make a sound. My skin should *pop* open, the liquid should *swish* around the barrel and *whoosh* down the needle into my flesh. I pictured the adrenaline-injection scene in *Pulp Fiction*, with Uma Thurman playing the role of my reproductive system. The physical, financial, and emotional toll of this process deserved a little palpable drama. Like many things, this daily act occurred silently, without a soundtrack commensurate to its importance, though its lack of fanfare didn't mean it wasn't actually happening.

No doctor ever determined any official diagnosis for my failure to ovulate regularly (so I named it myself: deviled eggs). In attempting to conceive our second child, John and I again took the necessary measures to shock my lazy ovaries and uncooperative uterus into behaving normally. Each month, as we decided, "Okay, yes, one more go," the lengths we went to grew increasingly dire: higher dosages, more shots.

This time, however, my body didn't react as well as it had before to the massive doses of hormones, and I ended up with a wicked case of ovarian hyperstimulation syndrome. The condition itself is not uncommon in women who have undergone fertility treatments; the severity with which I experienced it, however, happens in only 1 to 2 percent of cases.

Here's the not-too-technical explanation: While I had fertility drugs surging through my system, I successfully became pregnant. Then, the combination of the drugs and the natural pregnancy hormones reached a level that scrambled my brain into pulling some real nonsense moves, like sucking all the water out of my blood and dumping it into my abdominal cavity. Over the course of a weekend, my belly ballooned from its barely pregnant pudge to a beach ball. I knew I'd gone from feeling fine on Friday to feeling huge and out of breath by Saturday; what I didn't know was that my blood, now thickened by a lack of water, wasn't flowing properly.

If your blood can't circulate to your organs, your organs stop working. I didn't realize I was in danger of multiple organ failure, but I did make several calls to the nurse advice line over that weekend, in which I insisted something felt "not quite right." (Apparently good manners prevented me from saying "super fucking wrong.") The nurses told me to put my feet up and come into the office after the weekend.

I waddled into the clinic on Monday morning. When I sat down and opened my paper gown, the doctor looked at my stomach and I saw alarm flash across her face for a second before she composed her features and looked back up at my eyes.

"Okay, let's get you across the street now," she said.

At first, I thought, *To Burger King?* because that was across the street, but then I realized she meant the hospital.

When I got there, I had an IV line placed in my arm to replace my lost fluids; a hole poked just under my ribs; and a drainage pipe inserted through it. A bag attached to that pipe filled drop by drop with liters—LITERS—of liquid that looked like what comes out of rusty old bathtub pipes.

I stayed in the hospital for a couple of sleepless days and nights, with a constant parade of medical professionals coming in to check my vital signs. Then I got to go home, complete with a bag of needles, several vials of blood thinners, and a newly installed portable tap in my side, like a human keg.

———

In the chaos of that hospitalization, I didn't cry. I never said, "I'm scared." In fact, part of me was intrigued. When you grow up in a family of physicians, you develop a comfortable fascination with medical details. In a typical dinnertime conversation at our house when I was growing up, my dad might have discussed which patients that day had pus oozing from their surgical sites. I'm not grossed out by blood or frightened by beeping monitors or people wearing stethoscopes like scarves. I feel at home around people in white coats.

That's partially why I was able to focus mainly on logistics: Was someone at home watching our two-year-old son? Was I allowed to change out of this hospital gown and into a real shirt? What's the stuff being injected into my IV?

About a week after I got home, I was on the phone with my brother, a white coat himself, when it hit me how severe the situation had been (and maybe still was). I was sitting on the floor, my back against the sofa, the half-full drainage bag leaning drunkenly against my hip. My son climbed the cushions behind me, rolling a little Thomas the Train. I held the phone between my shoulder and my ear, so my hands were free to swipe the alcohol pad across my thigh, draw up my dose of blood thinner, and give myself one of the twice-daily heparin injections I'd sworn to the doctors that I could handle myself if they let me go home.

"You know, Mom and Dad were kind of freaked out," my brother said.

"Mom and Dad like to freak out. It's their hobby," I answered, stabbing the needle and depressing the plunger.

He paused.

"No, I mean—they thought you were going to die," he said, like he was explaining the plot of a confusing storybook to a child who didn't get it. They'd been discussing whether they should offer to help John raise our son in the event of my demise. I'll say this for my family: We're planners. *Semper paratus.*

He was right. It really was that serious. Intellectually, I knew it, but something in my head kept me from fully feeling it. I got a sense of calm from my wishful self-protection—like if I just acted casual, everything would be fine. If you've ever spotted someone creepy coming up alongside you in a parking lot and kept right on walking, polite as you please, you know what I mean. It's a mental trick: *If I start running, that must mean there's a reason to panic, so I just WON'T run, and therefore this situation WON'T be worth panicking about.* It's as if you think you can tap into an alternate universe by using the powers of your behavior, changing what is into what could be instead, taking danger right out of the equation. That doesn't work unless you're a wizard.

I acted as if everything was normal. *Just keep walking. There's nothing to panic about.*

I got to ditch my tap after a few days and quit the blood thinners after a few weeks, but as the pregnancy progressed, complications continued to arise. Month after month, bed rest after scare after bed rest after scare, it became harder to ignore my rising guilt. I'd brought this little life into being—insisted on it with ever greater scientific meddling—only for my own body to threaten it. I was doing everything as right as I could: drinking plenty of water, showing up for every monitoring appointment, exercising just enough but not too much, resting on my left side as instructed. Still, things kept going wrong. Bleeding when there shouldn't have been bleeding. A heartbeat that didn't sound the way a heartbeat should. I wanted to say to the doctors, "No, you don't understand. I've read all the books. I've done this before. I'm a *very good pregnant woman.*" Couldn't they see how I followed the rules?

In my eighth month, my perinatologist said the baby was in trouble again, because the fetal measurements from week to week weren't up to snuff. Was I eating enough? Yes. Taking my vitamins? Yes. Well, something wasn't working right, because the baby wasn't growing.

*"I'm sorry, baby. I'm sorry, baby. I'm sorry, baby,"* I whispered under my breath, tears rolling from my eyes into my ears, as the doctor pointed to the little creature on the ultrasound, curled up sleeping, probably hungry. Poor baby, stuck with me.

"If you can't get some weight on the baby," she said, "we're going to have to operate. We can't let this baby starve."

We can't let this baby starve.

I climbed down from the crinkly paper tablecloth, stood up, and nodded. Like a lunatic, I kept nodding as I pulled on my maternity jeans in the exam room afterward, crying silently and mouthing, "I can do this. I can do this. I can do this."

And so I drove to Piece of Cake, my favorite bakery, and picked out a "slice" of carrot cake. If you've never been to

Piece of Cake in Atlanta, what you need to know is that they bake enormous layer-upon-layer cakes that look like iced top hats, and then they whack them into—oh, about fourths, maybe fifths?—and box up the pieces. Those whopping wedges of cake shouldn't be single servings any more than a twelve-ounce slab of cow should be a "steak" for one, but if I'm going to bet my health and the health of my unborn child on cake, I'm not going to fool around with some flimsy two-bite cupcake.

I slapped that box of carrot cake onto the counter by the register and said, "I'll take this . . . and a fork." Then I went out and sat in my car in the parking lot, watching traffic whiz by on the busy road. I heaped a hunk of carrot cake into my mouth, clamped my quivering lips closed, and chewed. *Listen, baby—this is cake, and it has carrots in it, so it's also full of vitamins. It's like dessert and salad at the same time. You are going to LOVE cake. I'm eating as fast as I can. Hang on.* Forkful after enormous forkful, I chewed. I sat in my car and cried and ate cake for all it was worth. It was worth everything.

You tell me my baby will starve unless I pound some calories? I will pound calories like a motherfucker. You watch.


"She's way too small," the doctor said to my mother in 1975, examining my tiny body. "This is a case of *failure to thrive*." The way she recalls it, he wrinkled up his whole face and looked down at her like she was a two-dollar whore who had been starving her baby on purpose and using food money to buy liquor and weapons.

With the benefit of hindsight, we all know now that my babyhood was merely a preview of my particular body type. (I wasn't so much a late bloomer as a non-bloomer.) But my mom couldn't have known that with her first child. I was pale and scrawny, all white hair and invisible eyelashes and see-through skin over impossibly delicate limbs—the genetic opposite of my curvy, tan, brunette mother. Under the doctor's shaming gaze, she felt accused, defensive. So, as she tells it, she said:

*"Failure to thrive, my ass."*

I suspect time and my mother's flair for storytelling have streamlined this conversation, although I hope she really did say that.

Mom scooped up all zero pounds of me in my OshKosh B'Gosh romper, tossed me into the backseat of our Buick, and took me home to prove a point. Then she made a batch of homemade banana pudding. Not the kind that comes from boxed powder. The kind where you slow-cook a custard out of cream and eggs and sugar and then toss a few bananas and some Nilla wafers in it for decoration. For months, she fed me this concoction every day.

Now, before I show you the "after," I want you to imagine the "before." Picture the scraggliest little baby you can. Bony legs, stick arms, and a wild tangle of blond floss stuck on top of what must have been an awfully skinny skull for the doctor to be so grim about it.

Now.

Are you ready?

This is how the pudding diet worked out:

How glorious is that? Look at my grip on that bear. I probably ate him after this picture was taken. And look at my *HAIR*. It's like it saw how round my cheeks were getting and poufed itself up just to keep things proportional.

At my next checkup, the pediatrician said I was thriving quite well, and my mom—thank goodness—tapered off the banana pudding.

It was with that "*Failure to thrive, my ass*" determination that I loaded carrot cake into my face when my baby's survival was threatened. Such a small, simple thing to do—eating cake. But God, that cake was holy. I willed it to get where I wanted it to go, through me and into the baby. Take, eat—

this is my body and a huge dessert, given for you. This is the first of so many rituals I will perform to protect you. I will buy you fluffy shopping-cart seat covers. I will make you wear the biggest, ugliest bike helmet. I will secretly disable the radio in your first car and allow you to think it's broken, so you won't have any musical distractions when you start driving. I can't stop anything bad that might happen to you, but I will make all the motions, say all the prayers, eat all the cake.

It worked, for a little while at least. For a couple of weeks, John and I carried on the mundanity of life with our son—bath, dinner, books, bedtime—as normally as we could while I went on a linebacker's diet. I forced down giant meals of chicken potpie and milkshakes (urp), and at night we lay in bed, John's hand on my belly. "What's going on?" he asked. "I don't know," I said. I couldn't tell whether the baby was growing or I was just getting plumper from the steak and cake.

Eventually, the situation my doctor suspected was confirmed. My placenta had given up early and begun to calcify, cutting off access to nutrients. If we didn't do a C-section pronto, it would begin restricting oxygen, too. We had made it as long as we could. "Do you understand?" my doctor said, squatting in front of me where I sat with a monitor strapped around my stomach. "Yes," I said. "It's an emergency, but a calm one." She nodded. "That's right. A calm emergency."

We had twenty-four hours to get ready for surgery, and in that time, we rallied the troops. Our favorite sitter came over to take care of our son. My parents and my in-laws came to town. We made reservations for lunch the next day. That's the crazy thing about a scheduled C-section. You put it on the calendar, you go about your day, and then you just show up. There's no labor, no waiting around, no counting contractions. You can do anything you want before your C-section, really. Except eat. No food or drink before surgery.

So while the whole family sat around a table at our favorite neighborhood restaurant, ordering burgers and salads—and oh heck, it's a special occasion, why not? Light beers!—I sat alongside them, not eating. The mood was festive, and rightly so, as we'd been assured that waiting for an operating room wouldn't cause any further trouble and that as long as we got the baby out within twenty-four hours, everything would be fine. A baby was coming! But I felt detached from everyone around me at lunch. I could try to pretend everything was fine, but I couldn't convince myself the danger was imaginary. It was real.

I smiled and sipped water, thinking, *I will never be pregnant again. This is it. How many hours until we go? I am so hungry. My baby is even more hungry. My baby is starving and it's all my fault. I took all those fertility drugs and made this poor baby live in my stupid body that's not even safe. What if the baby's not okay? What if I had died? What if I could still die? What if this was my funeral lunch? Can anyone tell I'm thinking these things? Smile! That sandwich smells so good.*

There's a theory I have about why bad things happen. It's another little bit of wizardry. When something unfortunate occurs, I tell myself it's the less-bad thing I bargained with the universe for in exchange for something worse *not* happening. Like, if I miss my flight and can't make it on a trip, I tell myself that in an alternate universe, I made the flight but the plane was infested with lice and I got a terrible skin rash, and that I must have made a deal with fate that if I could just be free of my lice-itch, I would give up the vacation. Then missing out on a trip doesn't feel so bad. Or let's say I'm trying on clothes and feeling less than impressed with my pasty, flat-chested reflection in the dressing room mirror. I just tell myself that something terrible must have been about to happen in the alternate version of my life—like maybe some kittens were about to be hit by a truck while the busty, even-skin-toned version of me was out jogging—and in my courageous way, I said, "LORD, TAKE MY TAN AND MY BOOBS. JUST SAVE THE KITTENS." It makes me feel noble and empowered over my destiny. It's how I was able to stay relatively patient throughout the fertility process: Every time I didn't get pregnant, I was successfully avoiding whatever might have gone wrong in that pregnancy.

In that final twenty-four hours before I went into surgery, I tried to apply my mental coping mechanism, but the stakes were higher than those of any pretend-deal I'd ever imagined, and I couldn't follow my own hypothetical logic. There couldn't be

any bargain. Because in any deal, there's always the possibility that it will fall through and you'll get stuck with the bad end of it, the alternative conclusion.

There couldn't be an alternative.

As I lay on the operating table, pressed by heavy warming blankets, my arms strapped down and my body numb, the surgeons did their work on the other side of a short curtain across my midsection. I felt the bizarre, painless tugging—an understatement of sensation—while I watched the ceiling and listened to holiday carols someone had put on a CD player.

It was a few days before Christmas when our little girl was extracted from my inhospitable womb, a very reasonable four weeks before her January due date. Machines beeped, voices rose and fell, light glinted off silver instruments, and then a doctor handed her to John, and John held her up next to my face. She blinked. I blinked.

"You're okay," I said. We'd gotten what we hoped for, maybe even what I'd bargained for. There she was—healthy, if a bit lightweight, her skin hanging in little purple folds like a molting salamander—right there on the outside of me.

She weighed the same as a sack of sugar, five pounds, when we brought her home, but she ate enthusiastically and made up for lost meals quickly. Had she not, I was prepared to ask the pediatrician how soon babies are allowed to have carrot cake and banana pudding.

A couple of years later, she coined the phrase "me real," and it entered our family lexicon for good. We say it whenever we feel the need to push back against what's getting us down, whenever wishful thinking runs out and we've got to buck up and deal with the choices that are actually before us.

*Me real.*

# The Expat Concept

I was whisper-cursing at the oven when the doorbell rang.

At first I thought the *ding* came from the buttons I'd been poking on the oven's control panel. They were nonsensical pictographs, much like clothing tags that instruct you to "iron on low, no steam" by way of a diagram that clearly indicates "colonial hat, no noodles." I wanted to roast a chicken. My mother had come all the way from the States to visit us in Ireland, where John and I had moved with our baby daughter and toddler son, away from our home in Atlanta. His job had transferred him to Dublin, and we'd been there for just a few days before he had to travel again. He was in Brussels that evening as I searched the oven's dashboard for a picture of a chicken with steam rising from its body, or even one that vaguely suggested "heat" or "fire."

The doorbell rang again.

"Hello," said a young woman when I opened the door. "I don't mean to disturb, but there's a little boy leaning out of your top window up there." She pointed above her head. "And he doesn't appear to be dressed for the weather?"

Dressed for the—?

I leapt the stairs three at a time to the second-floor bedroom, where my three-year-old, unclothed and ready for bath time, had shimmied up the side of a bunk bed, opened a window, and begun grabbing at snowflakes and calling out merry greetings to neighbors.

"We don't stick our bodies out of windows, we don't talk to strangers, and we don't stick our bodies out of windows and talk to strangers *without our clothes on*," I told him as I cranked the window closed.

Everyone had told us it never snowed in Dublin.

I went back to the oven and pushed the picture of a comb hiding behind the sun. Nothing.


I had not prepared for this trip adequately.

If I could hop in that time machine and give my young-parent self some advice, this is what I might say:

When you are dropped off at your new front door by the airport cab with all your luggage at your feet and two small children clinging to your jacket and wailing, in the blinding sideways rain, you should *already* know where the nearest market, restaurant, pub, or food establishment of any kind is and how you're going to get there without a car. (Perhaps you were thinking you'd just yell, "Siri, bring me a dozen apple muffins!" But what if your phone died hours ago?)

Children who haven't eaten anything since the stale airplane dinner roll from the night before are no longer human. They are animals, driven purely by their hunger, ready to gnaw off each other's limbs and/or your face. And when you realize that you have nothing but three Goldfish crackers and some cracker dust left in a plastic baggie, and that the landlord who was supposed to show up with your key is nowhere to be found, you may begin to cry.

*Focus*, you'll think. *Don't cry.*

You may heave one big sob anyway. Because although you know you have absolutely no right to despair or exhaustion considering the world's spectrum of true despair and exhaustion—the wars, the famines, the plight of the animals nearing extinction—you also know now that you should have packed more granola bars. No one here is *starving*-starving, but your kids are starving, and no one here is *dying*-dying, but you are dying, and everything's soaked and there's no umbrella and the house is right there and you can't get into it.

*STOP CRYING.*

You will stop, but you won't notice that you've still got tears and snot and rain all over your face, plus blood streaming down your chin now from where the baby you're jiggling has just head-butted you and split your lip open. So it won't occur to you that you can't just knock on a neighbor's door and summon the last flickering twinkle of your Southern charm to smile and ask where the nearest grocery is. Because the neighbor might take one look at your bloody grin, mumble something you can't hear, and close the door.

But there's no time machine, so I can't go back and tell myself any of this. Nor can I ask my then-self: Girl, what were you expecting from this trip?

--------

A smart thing to do before going somewhere like this would be to connect with some people who live there—find a few friends-of-friends to show you the ropes. I didn't. In retrospect, I think it's partly because I was too busy trying to figure out whether a Pack 'n Play counted as a piece of carry-on luggage and if my baby could sleep in it every night for a period of several weeks without developing a bad back or whether babies even could get "bad backs" or if that's just an old-person thing. But I also have to admit I didn't think about needing friends.

Back home in Atlanta, I used to sit out in my little front yard under the shade of an oak tree in the mornings, just me and my little ones on blankets, watching cars and people and pets pass by. In the afternoons we headed to the park with other mothers and babies from the neighborhood playgroup. Most of those new moms had taken indefinite leave from work to stay home with their kids, and I, too, had quit my full-time job and switched to writing freelance at home. We'd had a couple of years of this routine before the opportunity arose to go to Dublin for a few months, and the idea of a change made it particularly alluring.

I knew this time of life wouldn't last forever, and sometimes I wanted it to slow down. Children of my own, time to raise them and know them—that's what I'd been waiting for, trying for, making deals with the universe for. When I held my baby to my shoulder after a bath, her warm, damp body wrapped in a towel, I thought, *I can't believe I get to do this. I can't* believe *she is mine.* When I attempted to snap pajamas around her roly-poly torso and found that they no longer fit, that she had moved out of nine-month-size clothes and into twelve-month sizes, I sniffled. I wanted, often, to freeze time, so I could hold my kids forever and soak up their babyness until it saturated me.

But this was true also: Our lives had a repetitive *Groundhog Day* quality to them lately. Wake up; feed baby; feed toddler; clean dirty dishes, dirty faces, dirty hands, dirty clothes, dirty diapers. Cut the same food into little pieces on high-chair trays, watch the same episodes of *Sesame Street*, play the same game of lining up stuffed animals across the den floor, every day the same, the same, the same.

I longed to mix things up a bit. I imagined, instead of sitting on our front steps, sitting on unfamiliar museum benches or in pubs, absorbing the conversation of our Irish neighbors, a world of train schedules instead of nap schedules. Wouldn't it be fun to have all the babyness and none of the boredom? A change of scenery always helps, I knew that, and although I couldn't picture exactly what the new scenery would look like, at least it would be different.

In Dublin, our rental stood in a row of identical old townhomes lined up like teeth on a cluster of streets rounded up behind a gate. Beyond our gate were more residential streets and, if you walked a little farther, a main road that stretched from one end of Dublin to the other. I knew we had neighbors, but I rarely saw them and had no idea where they went during the day. I never heard children, other than my own.

As the weeks passed, I began to venture out a bit more with the kids. I signed my son up for a toddler yoga class so that we'd have somewhere to go twice a week. While he ommmmmed with Irish kids, my daughter and I sat at an outdoor café—me sipping coffee, her mashing pieces of cookie between her fingers. We found a park within walking distance.

Once, I saw a flyer for an American women's mother-and-baby group. *Ah!* I thought. *Other parents. Fellow expats. Someone to talk to!* I took down the information about their next gathering and decided to go.

I had just started pushing my daughter's stroller into the loose pebbles of the hostess's driveway when a possibly rabid, definitely pissed-off Doberman came galloping toward us. My son, who had been walking at my side, screeched and climbed me like a tree.

"You should socialize him better around dogs," the lady yelled from her back door. "If you pick him up like that, you're just enabling his fear."

Her words enabled *my* fear. But I forged ahead, plowing the stroller through the gravel with my son perched on my shoulder like a baby monkey, the dog slobbering and pacing at our side. I introduced myself to a couple of people, and they nodded and turned back to their conversations already in progress. In the woman's living room, everyone was talking about a parade happening downtown later that week. One mother asked another beside me, "Should we meet there? Maybe get lunch first?"

That was my opening. I could have said, "Hey, can we join you?" Maybe it was the run-in with the dog, or the fact that other than yelling at me across her driveway, this woman and her friends had mostly ignored us, as if we were strangers walking past their private party, but shyness overtook me.

We stayed for about an hour. I stood at the edge of a few groups as my daughter sat at my feet and my son hovered at my knee. If I'd mustered a bit more extroversion I'd have gotten up the courage to ask a question or two. But the questions I wanted to ask seemed too big and unwieldy to inject into their conversations. I couldn't seem to get out, *How old is your baby?*—much less, *How are you different here? What will you do when it's time to go back? Will you go? Are you afraid?*

We didn't go to any more group meetings.

Babies need sleep no matter which side of the ocean they're on, so our existence in Ireland still revolved around naps, and the kids and I didn't stray far from the house for long. Because I'd put all my freelance work on hold while we were abroad, there was little distraction from the basic tasks of caretaking: making meals, reading stories, playing with toys, bathing, dressing, rocking. While—don't get me wrong— that sweet, loving contact is precisely what I wish I could get back for just five minutes now that my kids are teenagers who refuse to curl up in footie pajamas on my lap and let me read to them, it wasn't exactly a shake-up from what we'd been doing back in Atlanta.

And although it was a fun change of pace to see John more in the evenings (back in the States, he'd traveled so much that we often didn't see him for days at a time), he still traveled a good bit from our Irish home base. He woke early and went to work, sometimes hopping a train or a plane, and there I was, back home with the kids.

Our daily lives had not transformed with our relocation, except perhaps to get a bit lonelier.

I had not transformed, either. And I didn't realize, until that thought dawned on me with some disappointment, that I'd wanted to. I'd thought I might become someone a little more glamorous, a tad more interesting. But this time, a change of scene didn't change the whole movie. I was still pretty much the same character in the same film.

Looking back, I can see that when I had envisioned our life in Dublin before we left, it was just a concept, not a life. It included adorable vignettes like my baby tasting corned beef for the first time, my preschooler gazing contentedly out a train window at cows grazing in pastures, all four of us holding hands and skipping through fields of four-leafed clovers. It was photo ops, scrapbook entries, Facebook posts.

I want to fit into whatever culture I find myself visiting, whether that's a place or a group of people. And this desire isn't just about wanting to be liked—it's about wanting to show that I know the culture, that I've succeeded at passing as an insider. I have a new identity. This means that when I travel, I research the conventions where I'm going: What do people wear? How do they greet each other? Do they hold their forks this way or that? I can't stand the idea of standing out as a gauche American. It's just so lazy and rude—and wrong—not to at least try to do as the Romans do. Right? Unfortunately, sometimes I get so distracted by trying to mimic the culture correctly that I miss the forest for the trees.

John and I went to Italy once, years before Dublin, with two other couples. One of the first things we did after arriving in Florence was take a car out to an olive grove in Tuscany. We got to taste thick green olive oil on little shingles of country bread. I ate it up and memorized every fact our guides taught us. That way, at every dinner afterward, I could discuss olive oil brilliantly with waiters and enjoy it in an educated way. ("Mmm, definitely cold-pressed. They must be keeping it in dark glass. Great soil." What an asshole.)

One night we stumbled into a trattoria and were seated at a table in a crowded room. The waiter brought a bottle of olive oil and a hunk of bread. Noticing a little empty bowl on the table, we poured some oil into it and began dipping our bread. Mmmm, nutty? Fruity? When we polished it off, our waiter came back, chuckling, and offered us more.

We ate and ate, sopping up every last drop, wiping the bowl clean with our crusts. You don't want to waste that stuff. It's liquid gold.

It was then, as we sat back with bellies full of bread and oil, that I looked around the dining room and commented on how funny it was that in Italy people could still smoke in restaurants. We'd gotten used to dining in a haze. And then I noticed the smokers in the room—all at one time, seemingly—tapping their cigarettes into little bowls in the center of their tables.

We'd been eating out of an ashtray.


I'm not proud of this, but here it is: I put more time into planning my wardrobe for Ireland than I did into figuring out how we would eat. It was, in some ways, my first office job all over again—100 percent prepared on the clothing front, zero percent prepared otherwise. Okay, maybe I'm a little proud—I packed such good outfits for Ireland. Dark brown corduroy skirt with a jaunty kick pleat in the back. Knee-high brown leather boots with a low heel and a zip up the inner calf. Cream cowl-neck sweater, a thick, luscious wool blend. (I felt wool would be an important component of my Irish wardrobe, what with all the sheep we'd surely see roaming around.) In this outfit, I'd become a chocolate-and-vanilla-swirl, multilayered, luxuriously textured, cosmopolitan-yet-cozy quasi-Irish woman of casual elegance. I'd look the part.

I never wore it.

I never had the occasion. When I took the kids out on mini-explorations while John was at work, I pushed a stroller, wearing two layers of coats and an itchy beanie hat that kept my brain from freezing but mashed my hair into a sweaty mat upon my forehead. We stayed warm and had a good time, but we didn't look like a fashion spread. For the occasional big outing—to the Dublin Zoo, say—I had to swaddle my daughter so many layers deep in fleece stroller blankets that only her eyes and nostrils were visible. No one could see her parade of adorable ensembles, all color-coded to go with her big brother's sweaters, chosen in shades that would look great against a green backdrop, because of course, in the cartoon Ireland of my mind, everything was shamrock green. I'm not entirely sure I didn't see a little leprechaun dancing in the background of these visions.

It was not green in Ireland.

We got there in early spring, but it looked and felt like winter. Dublin was gray upon gray upon gray. Sidewalks and leafless trees and puddles on frigid streets. The air gushing out of the tunnels at the train stations even smelled gray. It left gray residue inside my nostrils that I blew out into a tissue every night. It *tasted* gray.

I sent email dispatches back to the States, telling rollicking stories about our adventures. *Here we are toddling down Grafton Street to St. Stephen's Green! Here we are on the windy beach at Sandymount Strand! Here we are in Howth outside a castle! Here we are celebrating Mother's Day with tea at Bewley's!*

These concept-life snapshots did happen. I was that expat American-in-Ireland adventuress, but only for moments at a time. "Look at this whole other life I have," I seemed to be saying to my friends and family, but I was back to being same-old-me by the time I sat down to email the pictures. I hadn't actually opened up a portal in time and space and entered a parallel life where I was someone else. This wasn't like that old Gwyneth Paltrow movie *Sliding Doors*, in which one person's life happens two different ways in alternating scenes. I'm a sucker for movies and books like that, because it's such a delicious idea—that each of us has enough potential to populate more than one life story. Somewhere deep in my twisted little brain is the desire to be so good at so many things that I earn the chance to be multiple people. It seems so unfair that we only get to read the choose-your-own-adventure book of our own lives once, that we can't pick a point and go, "Okay, this time flip to page 102 and do the rest another way." But no, I didn't have two lives unfolding side by side: Atlantan front-yard life, Irish train-station life. There was still only one me.

A special occasion, or location, or outfit, can give you something to remember and show off, but it's the everyday that makes up real life. The everyday is where we really exist, just the once, in chronological order. If you want to experience multiple lives, you have to cram them into that one timeline.

Our spring in Ireland had no denouement—no climactic event that shifted everything in our lives from one gear to another. I did, eventually, learn how to use the oven. I found my way around our end of town and signed up for Tesco's grocery delivery service. We discovered a neighborhood bookshop. We took a lot of walks. We loved each other on different ground, under the same sun.

That was it.

A couple of months later, John's job changed again and we went back to Atlanta, where the seasons had changed and it was too warm to wear wool.

# The Pros and Cons of Joining the Ruby Committee

I did it for the right reasons. And I did it for the wrong reasons. Both. Multiple things can be true about someone at the same time.

Did I want to do some good for the world? Sure. But also, I had been feeling invisible for too long. Really, it was that, as much as any do-gooder urge, that made volunteering sound so appealing.

What I wanted, after several years of staying at home, alternating freelance proofreading jobs with trips to the toddler playground, was a little more structure, a little more sense of purpose, and some acknowledgment from somewhere that I was important. I had not ceased to be a member of society just because I no longer applied a swoop of eyeliner each morning before I went out into the world and sat around conference tables where other people could see me. I could still make an *impact*.

When I went to parents' orientation on the first morning of my son's preschool, I listened to the instructions about book bags ("No roller bags, please"—which, seriously, who is sending their four-year-old to preschool with a suitcase on wheels?) and the rules about snacks (no nuts), but what really caught my eye was the woman who stood up and talked about the parents' association. All eyes were on her, in her shirtdress and flats, holding a clipboard full of sign-up sheets for various committees, smiling widely and introducing herself as "your point of contact if there's anything you need this year."

*I could be a point of contact*, I thought. *I could volunteer for something.*

I started small. Before I ventured into school volunteering, I tried neighborhood volunteering.

Green Ladies Garden Club members, mostly women in their late twenties and thirties, were inducted by fellow neighbors. Did I care about gardening? Not really, but this group was right there in my own backyard, and it had monthly meetings. Structure! Organization! Unlike some hoity-toity clubs that demanded proof of pedigree, the only requirement for this one was that you live on one of eleven streets that formed our neighborhood. By joining, I agreed to cohost one informational session about flowers per year. Cohosting duties included booking a speaker, making a casserole and a salad, and opening your home to the fifty or so people who attended. A few times a year, the club held fundraisers to pay for horticultural improvements to the neighborhood. Bake sales, wreath sales, that kind of thing.

I don't remember if someone asked me to chair the Pumpkin Patch Extravaganza or if I raised my hand and offered. I do remember thinking we could revolutionize the whole thing by selling not just pumpkins on the first Saturday of October, but advertisements on the promotional flyers that went into mailboxes in September. If we got local businesses to pay to have their names on the flyers as sponsors, we could raise even more cash for seasonal flower plantings! I presented the idea by showing off a sample flyer at a meeting in someone's kitchen one night. If I do say so myself, it was adorable, bedecked with little pumpkin drawings.

The assembled neighbors *ooh*ed and *aaah*ed as they passed it back and forth over bowls of chips and salsa. Then one woman held it up with a derisive chuckle. "Cartoon pumpkins?" she said, rolling her eyes. "So this is what you do all day?"

What I DO ALL DAY?

Has there ever been a more loaded phrase? I don't know what the right answer is to the "What do you do all day?" question. Maybe the right way to spend all day is hand-mashing organic fruit into baby food with a mortar and pestle. Maybe it's training for a marathon. But apparently it's not drawing cartoon vegetables.

I knew better than to care. I should have blown it off.

But I was tired.

And I was proud of my pumpkins.

Under my breath, behind a tortilla chip, I growled, "No, I screw your husband all day."

The woman who asked the question didn't hear me—thank God—but the friend sitting next to me did, and the tale has entered our book of friendship legends. Once every few years, someone brings it up. I remain extremely horrified (and slightly proud) of myself in that moment.

———

I graduated from neighborhood fundraisers to larger community events when I joined the committee for a party to benefit the local hospital.

The way big party committees work is this: You are asked to join at a certain level of financial and time commitment. If the event is to have a "bejeweled" theme (oh, picture the color scheme!), these levels will be named for gemstones: the topaz committee (you pay a certain amount for two tickets to the party, you agree to help lick envelopes, and that's it); the opal committee (you pay for two tickets and you make a small additional donation, plus you get invited to a pre-party); the ruby committee (write a medium check, help compile the guest list *and* lick envelopes, and you get the tickets, the pre-party, and your name printed on the back of the invitation); the sapphire committee (big check, more perks, name in a bigger font on the invitation); and the diamond committee (enormous check, a special gift upon arrival, and your name super-big at the top of the invitation ahead of everyone else's).

It's the second or third committee from the bottom you want. The opal or the ruby.

Why? Well, ask yourself this question: Do you want to throw a fun bash that raises enough money for a new ambulance, or do you want to throw a fun bash that raises enough for an ambulance *and* positions you as a good person in the eyes of friends and strangers? You definitely don't want to sign on at the lowest level (topaz, what a cheapskate) or the highest level (who has that kind of cash?). So it really comes down to how much it matters that your name be printed on the invitation.

I know. You're not supposed to want anything in return for giving something away.

But I picked the ruby committee.

If all I'd wanted was to give the city a new ambulance, I could have taken the money I spent on a dress and the amount I paid to be a ruby and made a donation. But that wasn't all I wanted. I admit it, I wanted my name on that invitation. Honestly, I wanted my name *anywhere*.

My name—all three words of it—no longer appeared on report cards or regular pay stubs. I did most of my freelancing as a ghostwriter, which means that after weeks or months of writing something, I'd see it come out in print under someone else's byline. My name wasn't even spoken aloud much anymore. (Think about it: Does a spouse or baby call you by name? No. That only happens in the outside world, the world of professional and social interactions.) I just wanted to see it in print—proof that I was still alive.

I still volunteer, but in less visible ways, for causes and people and organizations that need help I'm able to give. It feels better to me these days to give time and resources anonymously or near-anonymously. Still, I'd be kidding myself if I didn't acknowledge that even that kind of volunteering makes me feel like I'm doing something to make the world the tiniest bit better, which makes me a little proud . . . which just brings us back to wrong-ish reasons. Dammit. Here we are again.

I have, at least, grown out of needing to see my name on an invitation. It helps that I'm at a different stage in my life and in my career. My name is visible in lots of places now; I no longer need evidence of it in that way. But it's also true that my final major volunteer role just about did me in. So I guess I quit for some right reasons, and I quit for some wrong reasons, too. Both are correct, as is the fact that I'll never forget that last big volunteer gig: chairing the elementary school fundraiser.

It began with a phone call. Beware this call, the one from the acquaintance at your child's school who "just wants to bounce an idea off you."

Letting an idea be bounced off myself is how I ended up in charge of the whole thing. Not part of it, not one committee, but the entire one-hundred-person team of volunteers. And this was no pumpkin patch; it was an art sale that was expected to move thousands and thousands of dollars' worth of paintings, statues, and knick-knacks in order to finance teacher bonus funds, field trips, and classroom improvements. Heading up this organization was the kind of semi-full-time job that required apprenticing for a year beforehand in order to learn how it all works.

I got the call from the school's fundraising director while I was at home recuperating from dental surgery. I could barely form words, my mouth was so packed with gauze. She said, "I know you can't talk right now, so I'll talk, and then after we hang up, you can email me to let me know you'll do it."

Blood and saliva oozed from the corners of my numb lips as I listened.

"You're so good at motivating people," she said. "You're the most organized room mom at school—everyone says so."

Did everyone say so? Really? My ears perked up. I looked around my den, where broken crayons, puzzle pieces, and plastic doll limbs littered the floor, nestled among airy wads of shed dog hair.

It's a bit of a ruse, this seduction. It's like that trick men play on women sometimes where they say, "It's just that you're so good at laundry. I couldn't possibly do it as well as you can." That's bullshit. Anybody can learn to fold a shirt. Paying someone a compliment is just a way to psych them into doing something. And it definitely takes a bit of psychological trickery to make someone believe they want to take on a role like this.

Because it is a hard job—it really is. In this kind of gig, there aren't just committee meetings; there are subcommittee meetings and kickoff meetings and budgeting meetings. And preparing for each one requires forty-five trillion emails and phone calls and texts. I learned all this after I said yes—which, of course, I did. I fell for it, big-time.

There are also "staffing" meetings, where you have to decide which volunteers will be slotted into which positions. Who will be communications chair? Who can handle the finances? Who will oversee all the sales shifts at the event?

And here's the thing: Unlike professional staff, volunteer "staff" can't be fired, because they were never actually hired in the first place. In some ways, this is a positive thing. Most of the parents who gave their time and talents during the years I spent on this effort did so with the most generous of spirits, tirelessly showing up in suits and sweatpants and surgical scrubs and jeans to make phone calls and set up booths and smile at visitors. To this day, I love many of the wonderful friends I made during that time in the volunteer trenches. When something went wrong—say a batch of paintings arrived for sale without wires or hooks to hang them—these blessed souls showed up with drills and wire. When spirits flagged, they brought brownies and tea. They cheered each other on and thanked each other for help and made fundraising magic out of thin air. For the most part.

But you know how it is. There's always one or two. Or five. Or twelve.

There's always that volunteer who doesn't listen to instructions and therefore doesn't know you can't stack wet paintings one upon the other. There's always one who feeds off drama, calling separate "debriefing" sessions after larger gatherings so she can report on which fellow volunteers aren't pulling their weight and who's wearing inappropriately short skirts to meetings and, by the way, you-know-who's kid got kicked off the fencing team and *don't you want to know why?*

There's always one who breaks the heel of her shoe while working a single two-hour shift that you had to beg her to take so you wouldn't be short-staffed. She's the one who gets on Facebook and tells her five thousand friends that she'll never volunteer again because the event you just spent two years of your life planning is nothing but a nasty, dangerous yard sale. It's a colossal waste of time, she says, this event that you've poured your time into, that has filled your inbox to the point that you've long since abandoned your zero-unread-messages policy, that has required so many evenings of spreadsheets and slides and note cards that you haven't made dinner for your family more than once a week in over four months. This thing you've stuck with because you said you'd finish it and because sometimes it's kind of fun and because, mostly, it will be good for the teachers, and you're so, so grateful for teachers. What a shit show, the lady with the broken heel says, what an amateur hour. Everyone should just skip it, she tells them.

"I'm so sorry you broke your shoe," you have to say when you call her, which you have to do. "I know it's a . . . special shoe . . . to you." You swallow, willing yourself to keep your composure. "Would you mind, though, just as a personal favor, maybe taking that Facebook post down? You're absolutely right, of course, it's a travesty that your footwear was unsafe while on school grounds. But we don't want to upset any of our sponsors, you understand."

I'm not saying it isn't worth it. What I am saying is that you can't expect to give away your time and get pure, golden, ray-of-sunshine fulfillment out of it, no matter how glorious it may feel for a while to help a cause, to stand at the front of the room and feel seen and heard and able to make good things happen for people who deserve good things. Doing something for humanity doesn't mean you won't still find yourself sometimes hating humanity. You just have to know that going in. It's part of the deal.

The good news is that when it's all over and the last of the confetti has been swept from the floor after the party where you handed over the giant check and smiled for a photo, you get to pick up the phone one last time and call a bright-eyed mother of a kindergartner. "You've always thrown such good class parties," you'll say. "You're a natural leader. Everybody says so."

It's a little wrong of you to convince her it'll all go great; but it's a little right, too.

# Sports Radio

**My** friend Pauline and her husband had us over for dinner, along with two other couples—all of us longtime friends. After dinner, when the other guests retired to the den to catch the end of a football game, I went into the kitchen. After I finished sneaking the family dog a few bites of steak and loading plates into the dishwasher, I realized we'd stayed past eleven o'clock, so I walked into the den and said, "Hey, should we let these guys have their house back now?"

That's when everyone whipped around and shot outrage-lasers from their eyes: "Are you kidding?" they yelled. "Good God!"

You'd have thought I was standing in the doorway spinning a baby on the barrel of a gun. It was as if I'd shouted, "I LIKE TO BITE THE TAILS OFF PUPPIES AND USE THEM TO CLEAN MY EARS!" or, "I JUST SWALLOWED A LIVE HERMIT CRAB!" All these people I knew and loved glared at me with disgust and horror. I blinked in confusion as everyone turned back to the television.

"What?" I said to the room.

Only John responded. He patted the ottoman next to him. "There are two minutes left," he said. "And it's tied."

To say athletics are not my forte would be like saying a fried Oreo is not exactly a health food. As resolutely as I apply my mind to it, I have never been able to hitch on to the popular obsession with sports. If I think hard enough, I can almost understand why Judas betrayed Jesus at the Last Supper and how selfies became a phenomenon and why some men wear short-sleeved button-down shirts; but I cannot grasp why adult humans watch other adult humans run around grabbing at a ball, much less why our society agrees that the individuals engaging in this tussle should be paid millions of dollars. It's the gaping hole in my understanding of humanity.

The urgency of sports confounds me, too. The importance of whatever's happening on the field always trumps what's going on in real life. That's why I got yelled at for trying to leave a dinner party before the game was over. It's why you can't walk in front of the TV when everyone's watching the instant replays. It's why, if the score is tied in double overtime, you could skip naked down Main Street shooting hundred-dollar bills out of your ass, and no one would notice.

Supposedly, watching a sports game together is a social activity, but there's so much about it that seems antisocial. If I sit through a game for too long, I get not just bored and confused, but resentful, as if I've been lured into punishment under the false promise of a party. It starts to feel like everyone is yelling about offsides to test me, or worse, to spite me. It's like the universe is taunting me with nonsense just to see how much I can tolerate.

———————

In my late thirties, I noticed that many social interactions had started to feel like football games. Tedious. Pointless. Like a vaguely cruel act of aggression by a world that was rejecting me. At obligatory events such as parent socials and holiday parties I found myself lingering in parking lots and bathrooms, taking much longer than necessary to apply lipstick or check my phone. My fingers would curl into fists while I tried to listen to people I'd met once or twice deliver monologues on their house renovations, the weather, or—always the worst topic— traffic. Had conversation always been like this? Or were people suddenly choosing the most inane subjects to wax on about at length? Was I hiding my irritation, or could people tell I was bored to the point of hostility when they started in about how it was a bit chillier this week than last, or that February sure is a short month, or how did it get to be Friday already?

I went to another dinner party around that time, this one just for women, a girls' night out among friends of friends. Someone had been kind enough to invite me, and I was excited for the outing. Leaving the house at six o'clock meant hand-ing over the kids' dinner and bath-time duties to John, and an evening without that repetitive responsibility felt like a mini-vacation. I looked forward to a night among adults and anticipated the conversation we'd get to enjoy about books, movies, news, the secret to conquering migraines, war, secret grudges, and well, whatever. No talk about nap schedules, peanut allergies, or stroller comparisons—those were the things we talked about when children were around, when we passed each other on the sidewalk by the park or in a pediatrician's lobby. That was kid stuff. Tonight was for grown-up stuff. World stuff. Real stuff.

It began:

"Marge, you make the best chicken salad," one friend of a friend said, as we sat down around the dining table and shook our napkins onto our laps. Mine had a pastoral picnic scene on toile fabric, a Frenchman with a big hat and lace cuffs and a lady with her bosom tucked into a giant dress, both of them peering delightedly into a basket.

"You do," I said. "This is good."

Marge: "Well, you know I put grapes in it, that's the secret."

Person to Marge's left: "But do you boil the chicken? Or bake it?"

"Always boil it. Baking comes out too dry."

"And salt it?"

"Salt the water, not the chicken."

*Okay*, I thought. *That's enough about chicken salad.*

"How much salt?"

"More than you think. You want to be able to see it in the water."

"So, a few teaspoons, then?"

"At least."

"Do you use the light mayonnaise or the regular?"

"I like the light, but not the 'spread'—you have to get the one that actually says 'light mayonnaise' on the front. Don't get the spread."

Great, not the spread. *Now* we've had enough chicken-salad talk. Right?

Wrong.

"I'm doing the no-carb thing, though, so can I have that?"

"Mayonnaise? Sure. It's, what? Oil? Protein?"

"But is milk a carb?"

"Milk? I think so. But there's no milk in mayonnaise."

"Mayonnaise is dairy-free?"

Jesus H. Christ on a low-fat Triscuit. I looked down at the picnicking couple on my napkin and wondered whether they had chicken salad in that basket, and if so, whether they were anywhere near this excited about it.

"So you're saying shred the chicken, don't chop it?"

"Shred it. Always shred it."

Me: "Oh my God."

Marge and the person beside her looked at me. Had I said that out loud? I hadn't meant to be rude. But whatever mechanism I'd once had inside my brain that allowed me to tolerate small talk had broken. I couldn't pretend to give a shit about chicken salad any more than I could find the right moment to jump in and add to the conversation or change the subject. And the longer I sat there, frozen, the more irritated I became. I had to concentrate to keep from shaking my head, *no no no*, to keep from yelling, *SHUT UP SHUT UP SHUT UP*. The conversation shifted from chicken salad to organic soap, then to the best way to cut an apple. Fifteen minutes in, I wanted to scream, "Is anyone having some genuine feelings about something? Does anyone have something fascinating or funny or weird to discuss? Did anyone *do anything* today?"

John was already in bed when I got home. Taking off my shoes and earrings and flinging them on the floor, I whispered, "What is the point of having people over if you're just going to sit there and talk about *nothing* the whole time?"

I raged on. These women were smart, I knew that. They'd grown up various places, gone to different schools, had all sorts of challenging, interesting jobs. They watched the news. We all did. We all existed on the same planet as Beyoncé, Bill Gates, J. K. Rowling, and a million other less famous but still fascinating humans who were doing and thinking and making things. There was endless conversation fodder available to us, but their talk had turned as bland as an unseasoned lump of chicken salad itself. What the hell? Had they all suffered head injuries?

Something had changed these women from how they'd been before to how they were now. I didn't want to see it, but it was right there: They had become mothers. That was the connection that had brought us together—everyone had kids in preschool. I didn't know most of these people very well, but I'd known of them for a long time, in that way you're vaguely familiar with people your same age who live in the same place. I'd seen them over the years going to work, at coffee shops, at concerts, in the airport. Had they always been this obsessed with chicken salad, and were they just now seizing the moment to air their concerns? Or had starting their families caused them to shift their attention exclusively homeward, away from everything else?

*No*, I thought. I must be wrong. That can't be it. I don't want this cliché to be true. It's too silly and old-fashioned,

exactly the kind of stereotype that would get me riled up if someone else said it. This isn't something I believe. I *don't* believe women get less interesting once they have children. I *don't* believe being part of a family means you're not still part of the world. I *don't* believe caring about what you put on the table means you don't care about anything else. I don't believe any of that, but I'm seeing it, and I hate it. C'MON, gals, I need you to fight this tired old narrative with me. Please don't sink into the chicken salad. It's like quicksand!

I delivered this soliloquy with my toothbrush in hand.

John cocked his head, unsure whether or not to laugh.

I heard myself ranting. I sounded insane. Who gets that pissed off about an evening of dinner chitchat? There's absolutely nothing wrong with talking about chicken salad. Maybe there was something wrong with *me*.


Look, I don't want to have heart-to-hearts with everybody all the time. Anyone with even an ounce of introversion would agree that constant, deep conversation would become exhausting. Small talk has a function: to pass a short span of time with pleasant sounds instead of awkward silence. It would be unsettling and off-putting if someone you didn't know looked at you over their phone in line at Starbucks and said, out of nowhere, "Greatest joys and deepest disappointments of your past year, go!" or, "Here's a hilarious yet touching story about my parents that reveals my true apprehensions about growing old." You shouldn't do that any more than you should walk into

a party and yell, "I'M ALLERGIC TO LATEX—GUESS HOW I KNOW?" or "ONE OF MY NIPPLES IS ALWAYS LOOKING SIDEWAYS."

People who are good at small talk have a handy knack for greasing the gears of social interaction among strangers, and that's useful. I wish I were better at it, truthfully. But when small talk starts replacing real talk, you start to feel like you're among strangers even when you're among friends. I was in a phase of life that required a certain amount of socializing, floating around in blobs of people waving and smiling courteously. I needed my other interactions to balance those out. To offer some real connection, some meaning.

More so than ever before, I missed my college friends. Whenever I could, I schemed to go visit them or get them to come visit in Atlanta, so we could stay up and hash out life in brutal detail. I missed the debates in class and confessions in the dorms and dreams in the dining hall—and not because I missed being *in* college. I missed feeling *known*. I missed *knowing* what the people around me thought, wanted, needed. Whenever we got together, we clicked back into that gear, and our conversations hummed and sparkled.

I knew college was over. I knew that one of the reasons we talked so much when we were younger was that we needed to figure out who we were and what we believed—we needed to hear it out loud, change it a little, hear it again. I knew time was at a premium and life was more complicated nowadays; there was less time available for talking. But didn't the very fact that life was more complicated now mean we had more to talk about, not less?

———

I don't know that I've ever liked small talk, but I do know I used to be capable of it. I used to be able to *mm-hmmm* and *oh, really?* my way through anything. But now it made me want to knock over tables. It made me feel like the world around me was tuned to sports radio, and everyone but me knew what it all meant.

# Rock You Like a Hurricane

**Existential** spending doesn't really cure anything, but it's an enjoyable—if expensive—way to dilly-dally on the way to doing what you really have to do.

Having just finished a couple of big writing jobs and a volunteer project, I suddenly had more time on my hands than I was used to. The kids were getting older, too, spending more time at school, not depending on me as much. I felt like vapor in need of a shape to contain me. Who was I if I wasn't that person busy with a hundred tasks and a dozen phone calls to return every day? Who was I if no one needed me to make their lunch anymore? And what good was I—what quantifiable measurement could there be of my worth—without these value systems to calculate it?

These questions didn't excite me. They terrified me.

But rather than face that terror, I tried to ignore it. I told myself I felt antsy because I was bored. I probably just wanted to have some fun. *I deserve a break!* I thought. *This is what people do after a big job ends!* And because I am a relaxation-challenged soul who doesn't know how to simply unwind, I chose a mode of fun that also felt a bit like work: learning a new instrument.

I bought a guitar.

In another version of this story, the guitar-acquiring narrator might be a guy who'd been in a band in high school but then became an accountant who always dreamed of the parallel life he might have lived if he had followed his ambitions, so to reclaim his youth he goes and buys a Stratocaster and sets up speakers and amps in his garage, and now he plays "Come Sail Away" in there and cries. This is not that story. I had no rock-band past. My love of music has always been from the outside, as a fan. The only music I had ever produced growing up was as a classical pianist, and I'm sorry to say that I hated it. If I never play another piano scale in my life, I'll be damn glad. But I have always loved the feel of guitar sound vibrating in my bones at a concert. I craved the ability to make that sound myself.

Okay, I admit I did have fantasies. Not that I would be famous, more that I would discover some latent talent that would propel me into the social circle of the bands I listened to on the radio. I imagined Brandi Carlile, one of my favorite singer-songwriters. The first time I saw her play live, she wore a red bandana tied around her bicep and a black leather vest, and she had the voice of an angel who had just washed down a handful of gravel with a shot of whiskey. She was the human embodiment of cool, a model of courageous self-expression. So sometimes, when I envisioned playing my own guitar, I liked to imagine that if Brandi and I met, we'd find that we had similar artistic sensibilities. She would probably decide we should be a traveling folk-rocker-chick duo and I'd start wearing a red bandana around my bicep just like she does, and we'd be gritty yet melodic and everyone would love us and wonder why we hadn't paired up sooner. And we'd say, "Hey, it's like we were climbing two sides of the same mountain and we just met at the top." We'd write lyrics together, and Brandi would tell audiences how, while my guitar skills are indeed passable, what really makes this whole thing click is how I've helped her grow as a storyteller. And I'd say, "Oh, please. It's nothing." Everyone would chuckle and be enthralled.

That wasn't my *dream*, though. It was only a daydream. I really just wanted to see if I could play a few chords.

I did a lot of research in choosing my guitar. I didn't want some dinky thing that would fall apart, because I was sure that as poorly as I'd play it in the beginning, I'd probably break it if it could be broken. I also didn't want a pre-owned instrument, because the germophobe in me couldn't stand the thought of strumming strings encrusted with layers upon microscopic layers of someone else's skin flakes. So I quizzed my dude friends from college who were known to occasionally cry over their amps in their garages, and settled on a no-frills Martin acoustic. A review online billed it as "popular and affordable" with "classy looks." That made it sound like a homecoming queen, but the price was right.

The first time I lifted it out of the green felt lining of its case, I knew I'd done something slightly insane. I did not know how to play this instrument. I did not know how to tune or clean or even hold it. I hoisted it into my lap with my left hand, uncertain where to place my fingertips, resting my right arm along the smooth mahogany of its body. Was I supposed to cross my legs or leave my thighs flat? I inhaled and smelled vanilla, confused. Had I accidentally bought a scented guitar? I later learned that it's common for new guitar cases to be held together with vanilla-scented glue. At the time, I thought its strange sweetness smelled like a rum drink or old pipe tobacco. It didn't make sense, but it gave the whole experience an additional exotic allure.

After picking it up, smelling it, and putting it down for a few days, I finally packed the guitar into my car and drove to the music store where I had gotten it. I walked in, set my case on the floor, and pointed to it. "I need a teacher," I said, "and I don't even know how to hold this thing." That's how I found Robert.

Robert sported sandy stubble and a permanent case of bedhead, and his wardrobe comprised of jeans that looked like he'd worn them to dig a trench and a rotating array of Hawaiian-print shirts. To this day, I couldn't tell you his age. He might have been anywhere between forty and seventy, depending on how much of his facial creasing was due to age and how much to windburn and sun damage. When Robert wasn't working in the guitar store, he was driving his restored Trans Am—which I knew, because he often made reference to it and pointed out where it was parked outside. I suspect he fixed up that old sports car for some of the same reasons I bought my guitar.

We spent each thirty-minute lesson together in a soundproofed practice room about the size of a large refrigerator. The first lesson was boring, a guitar anatomy lecture. I learned the names of all the parts—neck, bridge, frets—and how a written chord looked like dots on paper. At the second lesson, Robert handed me a page of music. This was the first song he wanted me to learn: "Rock You Like a Hurricane."

I laughed.

I don't rock anything like a hurricane. I can't wrangle a supersize roll of paper towels without hurting myself. In fact, one reason I chose a guitar is that deep down, I really wanted to learn the cello, but I was afraid if the cello fell over, it would crush me and I'd die. This is what "irony" means, kids: wimpy me, a mild tropical depression at most, Rocking You Like a Hurricane.

But that was my assignment, and I applied myself to it. As I clamped the fingers of my left hand awkwardly on the strings and thumbed the chords with my right, the sound started to come together. This was no Brandi Carlile folk ballad—it was an '80s metal anthem by a hair band called Scorpions—but still. I was playing guitar!

Suddenly there was so much I wanted to know: Where could I get a book of more guitar music? What was the next song I'd learn? How long until I'd be able to play the guitar while also playing a harmonica strapped to my face like orthodontic headgear?

Robert said it just depended on how much I practiced.

So I practiced. Sitting out on the front steps of our house, I kept my feet supported at exactly the right angle. The sound, instead of bouncing off our kitchen walls, drifted away under the hum of Atlanta traffic. I whispered the lyrics along as I played, like I was in an old-school MTV video:

*HERE I AM* [strum strum, strum strum strum strum strum]
*ROCK YOU LIKE A HUR-RI-CANE*

I can only imagine what this looked and sounded like to passersby.

At the next lesson, I sat down to show Robert my progress. When I finished playing, he said: "Now do it again, but sit up straight and look up and out. You gotta stop looking down at your hands all the time."

"Why?" I asked.

"Because if you look down, all anyone will see when you're onstage is the top of your head," he said.

I loved how he bought into my daydream.

And I loved having a new hobby to pour my energy into. Maybe playing guitar could be what I needed to settle my anxious brain. Maybe if I had a skill to practice every day I wouldn't wake up wondering, *What now?* At the very least, if you only get to live once, you might as well acquire some new skills as you go. Learn an instrument. Add some grapes to the chicken salad, one might say. Try on a new persona. I've always loved doing that.

When I was eight, I begged my mother for one of those pre-made, all-in-one clown costumes you step into and zip up. This cheap-ass polyester number was garish, shiny, and came complete with a jaunty little hat and a palette of face paint from the seasonal aisle of the drugstore. I honestly can't believe my mom bought it, because typically when I begged for some flimsy store-bought thing she didn't go for it. But this time, my dreams came true.

At trick-or-treat time—that most holy of occasions when candy is allowed in massive quantities—I ran from house to house like a maniac. As is my way when I am on foot for any period of time, I tripped. But because it was dark, I didn't notice that my costume had ripped open at the knees when I fell. And because I was high on mini Snickers, I didn't realize there was blood streaming from both my kneecaps and splattering all over my shoes. I did sense that something on my legs felt funny, which is why I must have reached down to touch them a few times, which is how I managed to cover myself in bloody handprints.

I couldn't see myself, though, so I didn't know what I looked like. The only people who did were the ones who could see me—the adults who opened their doors and saw a tiny, tattered, gory, chocolate-toothed clown, standing under their front porch light, grinning and holding out two bloody hands. Good evening, folks. I've come to eat you alive.

When I was eleven, I dressed as Muammar Gaddafi. I made the costume out of a khaki outfit, aviator sunglasses, black boots, a liberal dusting of bronzing powder, and a very real-looking fake gun . . . which I carried with me to the festivities at school.

*What* was I thinking? I don't know. I remember deciding that the irony of scrawny little me going as an anti-imperialist, militant revolutionary with ties to terrorists was riotously funny.

And I know it fit my habit at the time to base a good bit of my elementary-school comedy routine on current events I saw on *NBC Nightly News*, which I watched religiously because I was in love with Tom Brokaw.

Anyway, I decided that's what I would be, and nobody suggested it was a bad idea. Not parents, not teachers, *no one* pointed out that my costume was about a dozen kinds of offensive and totally inappropriate for an eleven-year-old and for school. It was a different time, what can I say.

My first Halloween in Nashville working at the bookstore, just a few years ago, I dressed as the Girl with the Dragon Tattoo. I wore black leather and dark lipstick and moto boots and generally channeled investigator/assassin Lisbeth Salander impeccably, right down to the giant black, red, and green dragon an artistic friend drew across my shoulders. I felt dangerous, sexy, and completely unlike myself until the next day, when the semi-permanent markers ran in the shower and left me looking like the Girl with the Terrible Bruise for the rest of the week.

Obviously, time has not improved my costuming skills, but I still love trying on a different persona every now and then. It's a thrill to look in the mirror, blink your eyes, and see the glittery eyelids of a different person winking back. It makes you think, for just a second, *Who are you?*—which is a useful question to ask yourself from time to time. If you don't check in every now and then, you might not realize that the answer changes. So if you're feeling unsettled, I highly recommend getting a different haircut or outfit or eyebrow pencil (or guitar). It's fun. And who doesn't occasionally long to walk through the world as someone else for a while?

Playing guitar didn't transform me into a rock goddess, but man, it was fun. On and off for about a year, I took lessons with Robert. We moved from heavy metal into classic rock. (Turns out we didn't share much in the way of musical taste.) Eventually, our mismatched schedules made it harder and harder to book time together, and without actually meaning to quit, I stopped going, thinking I'd find another teacher with more availability. But when I stopped going to regular lessons, I stopped practicing. And when I stopped practicing, I stopped getting my guitar out of its case and smelling its weird vanilla smell. The calluses on my hands softened, then disappeared, my fingertips becoming tender again.

I still have the guitar. It mostly sits in its case now, although I do move it from room to room sometimes. When I look at it, I remember all the hope I placed in this instrument, how I whiled away so many hours with it, distracting myself with any music I could make. I remember thinking it might turn me into someone else. And I remember how good it felt to be in the presence of a believer—someone who said if you're going to play, you might as well take yourself seriously.

# No Safe Place

"I love lifeguards," I said to my friend as we watched our children splashing in the pool.

We'd recently joined a swim club not too far from our neighborhood, and I was happy for the kids to have a place to cool off during the blazing Atlanta summers. The pool also fielded its own swim team. I dreaded sweltering evenings waiting for my kids' races to come around, but I felt great peace knowing they'd have a daily swim lesson for a month each summer as part of team practice. They'd grow up to be safe around water.

My friend and I, mothers of kids the same ages, stood on the first step of the pool cooling our feet in the ankle-deep water. Though I wouldn't think of taking my eyes off my kids (ages four and seven) while they swam, the presence of a lifeguard added an additional layer of security. So much security, in fact, that on this day I wasn't even wearing a bathing suit. In white shorts, a loose yellow shirt, and a giant floppy straw hat, I felt I could keep watch from the edge just fine. The hulking lifeguards—young men home from college looking to make some money during the day before their restaurant shifts at

163

night—sat on ten-foot-tall chairs patrolling each end of the pool: red swim trunks, red foam rescue tubes resting across their laps in case they needed to offer emergency flotation, their heads turning slowly this way and that, scanning the water constantly.

If I miss something, I thought—if I turn away from one child for a second to look at the other—the lifeguards are watching.

"Will you send them to day camp next month when swim team is over?" my friend was asking. I'd been watching my daughter bounce up and down a few feet in front of me, holding her breath to crouch under the surface, then *pop!* out of the water like a jack-in-the-box.

"I forgot to sign them up," I said.

Bob, bob, bob she went, a little farther out, to a deeper part of the shallow end. *Pop!*

I looked at the lifeguard. His reflective sunglasses were pointed right at her where she bounced.

"So what are you going to do?" my friend asked.

"Hey," I called to my daughter. "Come back this way."

I called again, to her brother doing water somersaults nearby, "Tell her to come in." Neither of them could hear me over their own splashing.

Bob, bob, bob. A foot or two farther. *Pop!*

"HEY."

Bob, bob.

She went down. She didn't pop up.

She stayed down. This is what all the articles and safety courses tell you about drowning, that you'll expect it to happen with thrashing and screams, but it doesn't. It's a quiet slip under the surface.

I looked at the lifeguard, saw his glasses aimed at the surface where my child had gone down. He didn't move. Wherever his real eyes were looking, he didn't see her.

I leapt off the step into the pool. "GET HER," I yelled. To the lifeguard? To myself? My hat flew off and spun away, upside down on the water's surface.

I yanked my daughter up by the armpits. She choked and gagged, water streaming from her nose. In a second, the lifeguard was in the water next to me. "I thought she was playing," he said, his voice quavering. I still couldn't see his eyes, but I could see from his quaking hands, his rapid swallowing, that this boy, this other mother's baby, felt shaken by guilt and fear. He'd made a mistake. Anyone might have made the same one. It could have turned out so differently.

A few weeks later, I sat on a folding chair at a table near the pool, surrounded by other women waiting for our children to finish swim team practice. My daughter had returned to the water happily, her incident long forgotten (by her, not by me). We watched the kids do their laps, helped along every few feet by their coaches. In this instance, there really was no need to keep our eyes on them—the coach-to-kid ratio was absurdly high—although I didn't want to turn too far away.

So I sat and watched the little swimmers as people came and went in the seats next to me, starting conversations I tuned out. I couldn't concentrate.

"I can't believe it," someone said.

Did somebody get a tragic haircut? Did a toddler pee in the kiddie pool? Did someone forget to salt their chicken salad? What's so unbelievable now? I pulled out my phone to scroll through messages. I opened a new email.

*I'm sorry*, the subject line read.

It was from one of my best old friends, a guy I always called "the brother I never had." ("You have a brother, dummy," he'd say. "But he's the brother I *do* have, and you're the brother I didn't have," I'd reply.) We'd fought over something recently, the kind of fight where each party thinks they're in the right and that they'll make the other understand if they just type enough words to make themselves clear, but everyone only gets more hurt and offended.

I assumed *I'm sorry* was the beginning of his apology. But he wasn't writing to apologize. *I think we should get a platonic divorce*, he wrote.


Whatever unimportant thing we'd fought about in the beginning—some opinion we thought we'd shared but didn't ultimately see eye-to-eye on—had long since stopped being the point of our argument. Now we were arguing over our arguing: who was being unfair, who was being presumptuous and bossy. He wanted to take a month and not talk, maybe longer, because our last conversation had been so unpleasant.

"If you feel bad about yourself, that's not my fault," I had yelled. "Why do you project your problems onto me?"

"I'm sick of this. You're a vortex. You keep dragging me back into the same conversation."

"I AM NOT A VORTEX. I AM A PERSON. AND YOU'RE THE ONE WHO CALLED ME."

Had it really come to this? Could toddler-style squabbles actually lead to adult friend breakups?

Meanwhile, the conversation going on around me was picking up volume.

"I heard it was a while before anyone found them."

"It must have happened instantly."

I looked up, confused. "What?"

"Sarah's dad," another mom said, pointing at the herd of children in swimsuits huddled by the diving blocks for a motivational speech from their coaches. Sarah, the same age as my daughter, was not among them.

Someone explained that Sarah's dad—not a guy I knew personally, a friend of a friend—had been killed the night before in a plane crash. The adults were trying to piece together what had happened from fragments of testimony offered by people who had heard some part of the horror: A woman had come running through the pool gate by the snack stand yelling about a news story; Sarah's dad's best friend had screamed; another friend had gone over to Sarah's house to sit with Sarah's mom, who was, as you would imagine, in shock. From what everyone could gather, it seemed that after finishing up a business trip, Sarah's dad had accepted a colleague's offer of a lift home in a private plane. The plane flew into a mountain in the dark. No one knew why.

I listened to one conversation and held another in my hands.


"There was nothing anyone could do."

*I don't know what else to say.*

"Crushed."

Crushed.


I felt dizzy, sick.

Anything could happen. A child could slide under the water. Treasured friendships could end. A dad could pack up his briefcase to go home to his kids and have his bones and heart smashed instead. All this could happen right here in our world. The big sheltering umbrellas. The little spandex swimsuits. The towels smelling of bleach. The metal gate around the outside to keep strangers out and swimmers in. The cloudless sky.

I must have looked pale. One of the women at the table asked, "Are you okay?"

"No," I said.

My children were fine. My friendship was uncertain. (We'd resolve our issues over the next few months, retiring this argument to the Friend Fights Hall of Fame, although I didn't know it then.) Sarah's dad was not fine. Sarah's dad was dead.

Should I have snapped right out of my funk over my fight with my friend when I heard about the death of this man? It did put things into perspective. "Look, neither of us is going anywhere. We'll get over it," I said to my friend the next time we talked, several weeks later, as the ice began to thaw between us. But I felt like the tragedy should have made the squabble disappear, and it didn't. If anything, these two losses—so vastly different in scale—served to stake out two ends on the spectrum. That's one of the strange things about life: Even when we know how much worse it could be, everyday pains are still pains. Losing our patience, our dignity, or our good graces with our loved ones *hurts*, even if that hurt is nowhere near the grand-scale pain of losing a person.

Sometimes people say things like, "You think it's so sad that your kid is going off to college and your nest is empty? Well my cousin's kid *died*." Of course that's more sad. But one person's more-sad doesn't cancel out another person's less-sad. The fact that an earthquake took out a whole city block doesn't make it hurt less when you trip and snap your ankle. Your neighbor's cancer doesn't make it painless for you to lose your job. Sure, it might help you cope if while boxing up your desk you said to yourself, "This professional setback is nowhere near as bad as a tumor." That's what I do when I imagine that whatever I'm going through is the lesser curse I got in exchange for some worse outcome I traded away.

Bad things are still bad things, though, even if there are worse things. When you hear reports about the suffering people on our planet are going through—epidemics, drought, melting ice, corrupt elections, oppression—you might feel a little guilty for stewing over a disagreement with a family member or a roadblock at the office. But our personal concerns don't go away just because the world is going up in flames on a global scale. That's not how it works.

I once saw a flyer for a live storytelling series seeking performers. "No regular stories," it read. "We're looking for the extremes. The running of the bulls! The capsizing of the ship! The trauma you never thought you'd survive!" I like those stories—they're interesting—but I don't always want to hear about how someone faked their own death or escaped a fire. A sinking boat makes for a thrilling tale, but I'm also interested in how people deal with the sinking feeling of regret over an irretrievable harsh word.

That's what I thought about by the pool that day: Both types of sinking happen all the time. The thought had been bubbling under the surface of my mind in some form or other for a while, I realized. As my children grew bigger and pulled away from me, the less I could protect them. The more you have, the more you have to lose, which means the further you get along in life, as people and places and things accumulate, the greater risk you're taking just walking around every day. As a kid, I'd come to expect the unexpected—sometimes I faint, sometimes we move, nothing I could do about it—but now the range of "unexpected" seemed wider, scarier. One wrong step, and you could screw up something that could never be put right.

Was this the reason I'd started waking up with heart palpitations at 3 a.m.? Because I couldn't stop wondering who would be okay tomorrow and who would not? None of us will be okay, in the end. The not-okay is coming for everyone. It's a wonder we don't all go around with our hands clamped, white-knuckled, around the wrists of our loved ones. A death grip, indeed.

We act like there are safe places. We behave as though if we work hard and acquire the right things, gain the right access, put ourselves in the right zones, we can arrive somewhere where danger can't touch us—where anything *can't* happen. We pretend that if we can identify someone else's loss as greater than ours, we won't lose. But nothing really guards our lives. Lifeguards don't exist.

# A Letter to the Type A Person in Distress

**Hi.**

Put down your phone and Post-it notes for just a minute. I know you're busy rewriting your to-do list in your head, first chronologically and then in order of task magnitude and then visually like a pie chart with different colors for each slice of pie according to how long each thing will take. It takes concentration to keep the precision-tuned gears of your world-machine clicking along, but you can spare a minute.

I just want to tell you that your outfit today is spot-on. Are you wearing seasonal socks? Damn right you are. The rumpled, under-the-elbow half-roll of your sleeves didn't happen by accident, either, and I appreciate that. You looked up a video tutorial online so you could do it right, I bet. And before you closed out the video, I bet you left it a review. You look like everyone's favorite fun professor who's also in a band on the side and knows how to arrange a handful of flowers in a jar. That's a good look for you.

Not only does everyone find your appearance neat and visually pleasing, we all admire your words, too. Your emails dance on the line between eloquence and candor. You have a real sense for when to go with bullet points instead of paragraphs, and you're always handy with an emoji or a culturally relevant movie clip. Some say there's no place for exclamation points anymore, but you intuit precisely when to employ that unexpected little punch, and it always delights your readers. The note you sent to the whole neighborhood about the raccoon problem? Clear, to the point, but not bossy. The part where you called the raccoons "masked banditos with a taste for burritos" was a riot. Bravo.

The dinner you made for your book club last night had to have taken you hours to plan and execute. I know you left the packaging from the grocery store sponge cake out on the counter because you wanted to make your friends a strawberry shortcake they would love but you also didn't want anyone to roll their eyes and call you a perfectionist for making everything from scratch. Did you use a vegetable peeler or a paring knife to get the sides of the cucumber to look like green-and-white peppermint stripes? That was a whimsical touch and really added depth to the colors in the salad. People don't think about that sort of thing enough. You do.

I want you to know that I see your face when someone parks over the line in a crowded parking lot and inadvertently wastes a whole second spot, and I know your scowl isn't really about the parking space. When you stop to pick up trash on a sidewalk or put the to-go menus back in their rack at the sandwich shop, you wish you didn't have to. You'd rather everyone else pull their weight, but if they won't, you will. You like having work to do, but it's hard for you to work alongside people who cut corners and blow off responsibilities. It feels like they're doing these things to spite you, like they slack off because they know you'll catch whatever balls they drop. You can't fathom how they can feel okay letting so many things remain half done. This leaves you in a constant state of simmering, low-grade resentment, and you feel guilty about occasionally having the urge to throw your laptop at someone's face. You wish these things didn't get to you. You want to live and let live.

And I won't tell anybody, but I know you didn't really want to make costumes for the community center's spring musical. You don't even like *Mary Poppins*. But you filled out the feedback form after last year's play, because that's what you're supposed to do if you attend, fill out the feedback form. And because you were so detailed—that's what you should do, you should give details if someone asks for your input— they asked you to do the costumes this year; and you said yes, because that's what you're supposed to do, you're supposed to give help when someone asks for it—and now you're stuck trying to figure out how to make Mary's dress fit around the cast on the young actor's broken arm and you want the play to be great but you wish you hadn't said yes and you're mad that no one else said yes and that the same people always end up doing everything.

You wish you could take a break from carrying everything. It's all so heavy. You are so fucking tired.

I know.

―――――

And I know you can't help it.

I know that even if you wound the clock all the way back to the first time you can remember being this way—the moment you perceived that when you got things right, you got love, that when you achieved, you felt peace—that there'd probably still be no way to undo it. It's in your nature. It wouldn't matter if that moment or any other moment had happened differently.

You see yourself the way you think the world sees you, so you value yourself only when you are accomplishing and producing and finishing and succeeding. If you can't value yourself, then there's no reason to get up every morning, and if there's no reason to get up, then . . . what? You feel untethered, as if someone has turned off gravity and you've been spun into infinite space, a black hole that demands, *WHAT'S THE POINT OF YOU?*

It would be embarrassing to explain all that to someone, I know. It's awfully existential and weird to feel that if you get the punctuation wrong in a tweet, the world is a purposeless void. Not everyone gets it. So they don't get that if you worry that much over the little things, the big things seem so much bigger than they already are. It's bad enough wondering whether you've bought the right kind of sunscreen—are you living the right *life?* Should you change paths? Go back to school? Stay together or break up? Are you being the right kind of parent/daughter/sister/friend?

And I know that the more you do, the more it takes to feel like you've done enough. That's why you say "Sure!" to everything and sweat all the small stuff. Then you can be the person who gets the job done and saves the day and *then* maybe you can rest.

So let me tell you: I approve of the organic lip balm in the eco-friendly tube that you used this morning because it's good for your skin and also good for the planet. I saw that you waited at the four-way stop until it was your turn. I noticed that you RSVP'd to the invitations in your inbox promptly. Good work. You nailed it—all of it.

I know how much you need to hear this.
    I can never hear it enough.

# Stuck in Traffic

I sat in hours of gridlock every day, because although we chose to live in the middle of the city, the things we all needed to do—get the child's allergy shots, pick up Girl Scout cookies, fetch the special medicine for the old dog—were flung all over the metropolitan sprawl. I look back on these as "the driving years," and not just because everything and everyone was driving me crazy. To get one child to volleyball practice and another to lacrosse required an entire afternoon and evening spent in stop-and-go traffic, one kid always doing homework in the front seat while the other was on a field chasing a ball. The joke in Atlanta was that it took everyone a half hour to get to the end of their own street, but the truth was that most of the time it took twice that long to get anywhere.

I lived in my car, snacks and water stashed in the glove compartment because many days I spent so long sitting and breathing exhaust and staring at other cars' license plates—the automotive equivalent of looking straight at the butt of the horse in front of you—that hours would pass since I had last eaten or before I could give a hungry child a real meal. Watching a light turn from green to yellow to red to green to yellow to red while I inched imperceptibly forward just to get to the ramp onto the highway to *start* on my way to where I was going made me seethe with impatience. I growled curse words at the other drivers even when they weren't doing anything wrong, just because they were there. This happened for some portion of every day.

At home, when everyone was at school and I was not in my car, I got some sense of accomplishment from my work. I would take my coffee down to my office and open up a document to edit for a client, but although I loved the cleanliness and quiet of it, I felt cut off from the world, alone. The window looked out onto a gutter puking rotted leaves into the driveway. I had furnished my office with a "guest seat" in hopes that people might drop by in the mornings or pop in after the kids were down in the evenings for a glass of wine and a little conversation.

Coffee? I texted friends.

Can't today—soon! they texted back.

My friends were busy with their families, their commitments, their lives, and their driving. No one ever came and sat in the guest seat.

Life happens in phases, and even friends your own age aren't always in the same phase you are. With my babies now grown into big kids, I was ready to make more time in my life for non-child-related things. But lots of my friends were still having babies. Many were knee-deep in a phase of life that had the least possible time for other adults. But I felt like I was ready for my friends again, and my friends weren't ready for me. They couldn't linger over coffee in my office. They were still lingering over milk bottles.

I missed the sense of community I had back when I worked in an office with other people, so sometimes I crammed my laptop into my purse and drove to one of the hip coffee shops one mile (thirty minutes) away, where it always appeared through the big glass windows as if everyone was engaged in conversation, gesturing wildly and drawing things in notebooks. But my stupid giant SUV was such a tight fit in the Fiat-size parking slots that most of the time I got too nervous about hitting something and circled the block until I ran out of energy and went home.

I started sitting at my kitchen island during the day, scrolling through Twitter, staring out the window, avoiding going downstairs to get to work. I let deadlines slide while I sat around thinking up metaphors for what I felt like. Here's one: My daily existence felt like a skin mask—the kind that comes in a jar and smells like flowers and sugar when you smooth it across your cheeks and forehead and chin, creamy and slick at first. Then it dries, and as it shrinks up, it tightens and sucks the moisture right out of your pores. It cracks and puckers around your eyelids so you can't blink, and the only thing you can think about is that you must get it off right now, you must catch one flaky edge with your fingernail and peel it off—rip it off!—so that your skin can breathe again in the moist, warm air.

Here's another: Imagine you had a sweater in your size, in the exact color you liked, in the cotton blend that slides softly over your arms as you pull it on each morning. And you wore this sweater every day, and it was the very best sweater, and then one day, something happened—you don't know what,

because you don't recall putting it in the dryer or washing it in hot water—but now it is just enough too tight that the fabric bunches up around your rib cage, the seams itch, and you can't lift your arms over your head. You wonder if you've somehow put it on backward, so you try to take it off and put it back on the right way, but you just get stuck in it more, and now your elbows are pinned to your face and there's a sleeve over your mouth, and you're in a full, smothered panic.

That's what I felt like, but worse, and all the time. Something had fallen out of place in my head. Sometimes I had heart palpitations so violent I could see my chest flutter through my shirt, brought on by nothing at all. And when I didn't feel that anxiety, I didn't feel much of anything. I often thought, *Shit, what right do I have to feel this way? It's so stupid.* I told myself to get over it, because people were depending on me. So I decided to keep going and doing the things I signed up to do, because it's wasteful and self-indulgent to feel bad when so much is really quite good. It's ungrateful, and I was *not* going to be ungrateful.


But I didn't do a great job of "keep going."

I didn't answer my phone or check my voice mail.

I didn't change out of pajamas during the day.

I saw no point in washing my hair.

I sat in my car in the parking lot by the soccer fields instead of getting out and waiting with the other parents.

I thought about sleep all the time. Some mornings, I could not fathom how I would get out of bed, even though the world

that waited for me was beautiful and full of people I loved. When I was awake, I wished for sleep, and when I was asleep, I dreamed about being dead. Not about actually killing myself or getting hit by a train or anything that dramatic, just being *not alive*. What was the point of waking up?

One night after the kids were asleep and while John was traveling for work, I opened a bottle of prosecco and drank the whole thing, sitting on my sofa by myself, pouring glass after glass into my favorite champagne flute—the one with little etched bubbles on the glass. (This is the ladylike version of pounding whiskey.) Life is short! Why not! This is a beverage I enjoy! I swallowed sip after fizzy sip, trying to feel something.

I woke up at 3 a.m. feeling like I had rubber bands knotted around my intestines, cold sweat soaking my hair, pajamas, and pillowcase. *That was dangerous*, I thought, *sitting there drinking like that*. I'm always tipsy after a glass and a half—no wonder I felt like a tank of pressurized vomit after a whole bottle. I was the only parent at home, and I got all-out drunk. *I am a horrible mother. I am dangerous. What is wrong with me?*

I stopped being on time—for anything. My whole life, I'd always arrived compulsively early. Suddenly I was the one always running behind. Or, if I did show up on time, I left some essential element at home—I'd make it to a meeting but forget all my notes. Whole chunks of my calendar slipped my mind.

On the first day of first and fourth grade for my kids, I forgot to pick them up.

The teacher on carpool duty called my cell phone at four o'clock (they got out at three) and said, "So . . . are you . . . coming?" I didn't forget I had kids, I swear—I love my kids (is it ridiculous to have to say that?)—but I was getting worse and worse at keeping track of where we all had to be and when.

I often explained my frazzled lateness by saying, "Sorry, I'm trying to be three people." I blamed my lost punctuality on the difficulty of juggling our calendars.

It wasn't just that, though. I was distracted by more than the frenetic schedules of our household. All the other people I'd been and not been in my life were beginning to fight for their share of my brain space and their chance at a breath of real-life air, too. There were far more than three people crowded into my head. I felt like a human traffic jam.

# Diane von Furstenberg's Apartment

**We** always hurt the ones we love, the song says. Why? Because they're there.

My therapist said I was depressed. And when I got depressed, I turned into a truly worthless spouse. It wasn't that I blamed John for how I felt. But I couldn't separate him from it, so I thought I needed to separate myself from him. Sweet John, who started doing all the laundry when he noticed I'd quit paying attention to the growing mountains of dirty clothes. Kind John, who brought home cupcakes when my doctor prescribed them (in addition to Zoloft). She said I should savor the positive sensation of slowly chewing a food I liked. He stood in the kitchen and watched as I rolled a bite of cake around in my mouth in exaggerated, cartoonish slow motion. "Are you savoring the sensation?" he asked. "I think so," I said with a mouthful of thoroughly chewed cake.

"What if," I asked after I swallowed my cake, "I got out of here?" I gestured widely, indicating that "here" was at least the kitchen, and probably the rest of the house.

"What do you mean?" he asked.

"Diane von Furstenberg and her husband keep separate apartments in Manhattan. Maybe we could do that."

"Live in Manhattan?"

"Live separately."

"Hmm."

That's where you'd expect someone to go, "*What?*" or to slam his glass down on the counter in shock or outrage. But big conversations like these are where the differences in our personalities really show. If someone says to me, "I need a break from you," I immediately think, *So you hate me? You never want to see me again? We're ALL GOING TO DIE ALONE?* Not John. He pauses. He thinks. He asks for clarification.

We had an hour-long discussion in which I tried to describe what I thought I meant, making it up as I went along. "Okay, what about this . . ." I kept saying, summoning every last scrap of my problem-solving, can-do attitude as I outlined imaginary logistics: co-parenting our children but with nights off for each of us, staying married and devoted to each other, but living in different homes. In the scenario I envisioned, John and the kids would stay in our house, with me in a smaller house or condo around the corner. Or maybe we'd take turns in the kid house. Maybe both houses would be the kid house? Walkable to each other, definitely. Next door? The more I talked about it, the more I wondered why all married people with kids didn't keep two homes. Surely everyone wanted their space sometimes.

We had the conversation again the next day, and then again a week later.

"But . . ." John said, choosing his words carefully, "I don't want you to leave me."

"I wouldn't be leaving you," I said. "Just having a separate space. I'd still be *with-you* with you."

"But everyone would think we were separated." He was thinking through every angle. What it would mean for us, but also what it would mean for people around us. How much gossip would we have to deal with?

"And we could say, 'Fuck you, everybody, it's not your business,' because *we* would know we were still married."

"Would we need . . . another sofa? Two of everything?" Bless his practical soul. At no point did he panic. At no point did he raise his voice or call me insane.

He did want to know how we'd explain it—or would we explain it?—to parents and in-laws. "So when your mom comes to visit, you'd just act like you lived here?" he asked.

"Well, I don't know. I don't want to make the kids lie." This was getting complicated.

"They'd be the only kids in school with still-married parents who live in separate houses."

"Would they?"

If someone were watching us have this conversation without sound, it would probably look like we were talking about what kind of takeout to get for dinner.

I kept thinking, *I don't belong here, I need to get out*, and I wanted space desperately, but as I tried to bring this hypothetical scenario into focus, I understood that I didn't really want to be without John. I didn't really want to be without our children. I wanted to step out of my everyday somehow—to hop in my time machine and let it lift me out of my life for a while—but I wasn't able to translate this desire into anything realistic. I wanted to get "away" the way you tell someone to "go away" when you're little and you don't want to play with them anymore; and the person I didn't want to play with anymore wasn't John, but myself.

When you say "Go away," you don't care where the person goes, you just want them out of your sight. I wanted to put myself out of my own sight—out of my own regular life. I'd become an angry person who cursed at cars on the highway, a sad person who sat and stared out windows. I didn't know how to fix myself, so I wanted to step away from the story in which this self was the main character.

But I couldn't make a good guess at what "away" might look like. The idea of setting up separate households unraveled before it ever came together. John listened as I talked about it for several days, before eventually I let it go. It made no sense.

(I shouldn't be surprised Diane von Furstenberg's living arrangement didn't fit me. Her wrap dresses never have either.)

Instead of thanking John for his patience and support throughout the months when I slumped like a sandbag on various pieces of furniture and made few, if any, useful contributions to our household, I often snapped at him. I blew up over tiny things. ("WHO PUTS A BOWL IN THE TOP RACK OF THE DISHWASHER?") As I tried to pin my unhappiness to some cause, I made various arguments in which he'd have to share blame: Was I the beleaguered spouse, forced to give up her dreams and run carpools all day? No. No one forced any of my professional decisions, and if I wanted to change the carpooling schedule, nothing was stopping me. Was I tied down to domestic life, inhibited from a life of desert roaming and deep-sea fishing because I had children to drive around town? No. I mean, I did have children to drive around town, but (a) I wanted children. No one just handed me kids I didn't want to raise. And (b) I knew damn well that left to my own devices, I don't really do any deep-sea fishing or desert roaming. None of it added up.

Still, my mind tried to find ways to resent him, because he'd been there all along, part of every adult decision I'd ever made. If I was miserable where I'd ended up, wasn't that a little bit his fault?

One evening, waving the paper towel I'd just torn off to wipe the countertops, I said, "I mean, what if I wanted to go bungee jumping tomorrow? I have meetings! I have carpool! I couldn't even go!"

"Do you want to go bungee jumping?" he asked.

"No. The point is EVERYTHING HERE IS KEEPING ME FROM BUNGEE JUMPING. Why aren't you listening?"


We go through life looking for proof that our choices have been right. Psychologists call this confirmation bias. If you're a scientist, confirmation bias in experiments can lead to errors, because without realizing it you give greater weight to any findings that support your hypothesis and make excuses for findings that don't. You draw faulty conclusions, because you're not being objective.

In our personal lives, we also look for proof that our choices have been right. Even when it comes to small everyday decisions, we can talk ourselves into justifying a wrong as a right, because that feels better than saying we were wrong. (How many eyeshadows do I own that make my eyelids look like gilded lizards? Several. But I don't get rid of them, because I've already bought them and I don't want to believe I wasted my money.)

Here's the problem with taking that approach to life all the time: It's totally normal to look around every now and then and see that some things aren't working—that you need to adjust the dials, retool your life a bit. That's what people do. But you have to overcome confirmation bias in order to do that. You have to be willing to call something wrong, to say something feels bad. That's hard enough for any human being. For me, a person whose very identity and peace rely on looking at things and thinking, *Yes, that's right*, looking at my own emotional state and feeling, *No, that's wrong*, was more than unsettling. It felt disproportionately catastrophic. It made me think, *Wait, if I'm not the person who makes the right choices all the time, then who am I?* That I might have made choices that were "right" at one time but feel "wrong" right now seemed impossible. Right choices are supposed to feel right forever . . . right?

Wrong is the one thing I cannot stand to be.


I knew in my bones that John was not the problem. But I took my discontent out on him because he was the closest person to me. Because he could see how messed up I was, I became even more aware of how messed up I was. He pulled me close, but when I looked into his eyes all I saw was my own warped reflection. I imagined how grotesque I must seem.

When I look back now at this time when I craved solitude and escape, I see that I wanted to be unwitnessed for a while, that's all. I didn't want anyone to see how wrong I felt. I wanted a chance to feel messed up without also feeling self-conscious. It was like the feeling I used to get before I fainted—an inkling of a crash, a hunch that I should get close to the ground. I needed a place where I could hit the floor without the added anxiety of knowing someone was watching me fall.

# Nora Ephron and the Lives of Trees

**There's** a line in Nora Ephron's autobiographical novel *Heartburn*—"Show me a woman who cries when the trees lose their leaves in autumn and I'll show you a real asshole." I read the book for the first time in seventh grade (not exactly age-appropriate) and again as an adult, which is when I thought, *Wait a second—I cry sometimes when leaves fall.* I've also been known to get a little teary when I see a craggy pebble that looks like a frowning face. I sniffle when I see a skunk in my yard who looks lonely, like it's dawning on him that all his skunk friends went on an adventure and purposely didn't tell him where they were going. I laugh, too—like when I see a twig that looks like it's giving me the finger. I chuckle when I see an ant trying to carry half a Froot Loop.

I like to draw birds and jellyfish and flowers wearing hats, and very often these creatures feel as real to me—and as filled with inner narratives—as people. This is true of me now and it was true of me as a child, when I doodled puppies on every piece of paper I passed. I have always seen animals as characters. The way some people stop at every stroller to coo over a baby, I stopped to pet dogs. I imagined backstories for every canine I met. Seeing a dead dog on the side of the road undid me for days (and still does). I couldn't turn it off, the imagining, so I'd envision everything that led up to the dog's tragic quest. What compelled him to go into the street? What was he seeking? Maybe he wandered off in search of a snack. Maybe he was tired of his neglectful family and his concrete kennel. Maybe he just wanted some exercise. Maybe he saw a bird.

As a cartoonist, I use my imagination to bend the light of humanity through the prism of the natural world. A drawing of a penguin who's mad because the self-tanner she bought doesn't give her the even bronze glow it promised makes you think, *That's ridiculous*. And it's not ridiculous just because penguins don't use self-tanner. It's ridiculous because a tan is a goofy thing to get so angry about. It's silly when a penguin does it, and it's just as silly when a person does it. Projecting our foibles onto other creatures helps us get perspective and laugh at ourselves.

I shouldn't care what the late Nora Ephron would have thought of me. It's not like we were friends. She was old enough to be my mother, but she was not my mother—or my aunt or my cousin or anyone with any connection to me. But we people-pleasers want to be liked, even by people we've never met, especially by people we admire. How many times have I seen *When Harry Met Sally*? More than I could ever remember or count. Oh, how I marveled at the words Nora Ephron put into Meg Ryan's and Billy Crystal's mouths. What a genius she was. I wish she were still alive, so I could explain to her how much I loved her work and also how wrong she was about this one thing.

The other day I watched a video of a helicopter rescuing a cow in Italy. The cow had gotten stuck in a ravine and she—he? I can't call animals "it"—couldn't scale the walls to get out. Of course she couldn't. She's a cow. Cows can't climb. But do they know they can't climb? Did that cow panic? A veterinarian friend of mine says animals don't dwell on the past and future. They live in the moment. This is why it's so kind and responsible to put a dog to sleep when it's in pain from a terminal illness. The dog doesn't think, *I want to stay alive long enough to see the snow fall one more time*. The dog just feels that his legs hurt, that he cannot get up onto his favorite chair, that he is vomiting again. That cow wasn't thinking ahead to her demise and worrying about whether her family would miss her, nor did memories from her calf-hood flash before her eyes. She just knew she was stuck.

After the rescuers hitched her into the harness and took off in the helicopter, what must have gone through her mind? A cow has no instinctive concept of what a helicopter is. *WHAT THE FUCK IS THIS?* she must have thought, as the propeller chopped through the air. I can only imagine what the cow made of flight, as her feet left the ground and her view of the familiar meadow tilted and widened.

We all know animals have emotions and personalities. There's plenty of science to back that up, not to mention anecdotal evidence all around us. There's a squirrel in my yard who shoves all the other squirrels out of the way at the bird feeder. He's a bully. Dogs and cats and other animals can have anxiety, depression, even OCD. Just ask my yellow mutt, Woodstock, who can't sit down until he turns around forty-five times and who, once he sits down, licks his own paws until one of us places a hand on his head and says, "Enough."

In his book *The Inner Lives of Animals: Love, Grief, and Compassion*, the German forest ranger Peter Wohlleben proves himself to be a kindred spirit. He believes animals have souls. Not just the animals with cute, furry faces, like deer and goats, but the less cuddly ones, too: ravens, caterpillars, and ticks. I found it a compelling read, but anyone who finds it a bit twee would probably raise their eyebrows even higher at his prior book, *The Hidden Life of Trees: What They Feel, How They Communicate*. In that one, Wohlleben envisions trees in a forest as "friends" and "families" who share root systems and adjust their branches to make sure their neighbors are getting plenty of sunlight. He posits that trees can get scared and have memories and that they talk to one another through electric signals sent via the "Wood Wide Web."

It's an anthropomorphized view, certainly, but everything he describes has at least some basis in scientific fact. Acacia trees, for example, warn other nearby trees when grazing giraffes come around. The trees give off a gas that other trees can sense, prompting those trees to produce a substance in their leaves that makes them less desirable to snacking wildlife. Perhaps it's a stretch to say that this is proof that trees feel fear. But Wohlleben writes that when he speaks of trees in this way, people's eyes light up. He has translated the nonhuman parts of our environment into terms humans relate to, by making those things seem more like humans themselves.

Talking about animals and plants this way makes us feel less alone as living creatures, too. It's soothing, isn't it, to think of trees loving their parents, caring for their neighbors, and raising their babies? We all want the same things: to survive, to grow, not to be left behind.

I know I'm not the only one who thinks like this. If I were, animal videos wouldn't go viral like they do. At the time of this writing, Batzilla the Bat, the Facebook page of a bat sanctuary in Australia—where I have never been but whose online presence I follow religiously—has nearly three hundred thousand followers. These people, including me, follow along to find out who's new in the sanctuary and how they're doing. The people who run the Facebook page give all the bats names and stories:

*"Rescued a couple of weeks ago after being found flapping around in the middle of the road, Mr. Parfrey was in deep trouble, but following bed rest and time in care, he was joyfully released back to his home camp this afternoon."*

When I watch a video of a baby bat being swaddled in a washcloth or having his face wiped down with a Q-tip, it is not because I want to be wrapped in a washcloth and have my face swabbed down (whoa, claustrophobia), but because I feel for that bat. He is not alone, and I am not alone. There's comfort in that.

When I get lost in the imagined thoughts of a cow flying over a ravine, I am taking that comfort: Look, we all get scared. We all look around at the world these days and wonder what the fuck. Just as there are many things about humans that cows cannot understand, such as helicopters and artificial flight, I suspect there's a lot about their lives that escapes our comprehension as well. We're all a little confused about each other most of the time. That's probably why instead of curbing my animal-drawing habit when I grew up, I drew more and more the older I got. Is it weird that a full-grown woman published a whole book of cartoon birds experiencing botched social interactions, existential dread, and petty grievances? Or does it make perfect sense? The latter, I say.

So yes, ghost of Nora Ephron, when fall comes and the world turns cold and inhospitable, I cry. Because everything in nature decays. And if there's humanity in nature, well then, there's nature in humanity as well. If everything dies, then *everyone* dies, and that means my family and my friends and me, and guess who else? Nora Ephron, that's who. You're not even here to call me an asshole, Nora. We never even met, and now you're gone. Just like the leaves in November.

I think she would have understood, I really do.

# This Is Not My Cat

"**Come** out slowly and show yourself," I said into the darkness. I crouched on the floor, holding up the white cotton dust ruffle with one hand and squinting into the dark cavern under the bed. My nostrils and lungs registered the presence of fur, but my eyes detected nothing. The black cat, hiding motionless, did not want to be found, but it was my job to feed him. I needed him to give up his antisocial ways and accept a dish of Fancy Feast, but I also didn't want him to come bolting out like a hell-monster and scratch off my face. My understanding of feline behavior was founded on very little. I'd been allergic to cats all my life, but I suspected—based on legends, internet memes, and that one pesky neighbor years ago—that all cats were pricks.

"Fine, then. *I'm* going to have some Savory Salmon Feast." I could wait him out. There was no rush. In the three weeks that lay ahead of me in this house-sitting gig, he'd have to get hungry eventually. I went into the kitchen and surveyed my own stash of groceries, lined up on the butcher-block counter: a can of almonds, a bunch of bananas, two cases of lemon-flavored fizzy water, a bag of Mint Milano cookies, a box of Triscuits, and a tub of pimiento cheese. All the food groups, plus a bottle of anti-depressants and some Claritin for the cat allergies.

I don't cook when I'm on my own. I graze. It's one of the small measures of tenderness I grant myself, the removal of all pressure to feed and water fellow humans. The only creature other than myself I had to keep alive that summer was the cat. He came with the house.

To let the cat know I was still around, I took a stroll through this home that wasn't mine. There was a portrait of a young woman I'd never met, her dark hair falling over the lace neckline of a white dress. There was that woman's bedroom. The sunroom. A little wooden deck. A row of plants I was expected to hose down periodically so their leaves wouldn't scorch in the July sun.

I stood on the deck and pulled up a map on my phone to get a better feel for where I was in relation to the rest of the city. I visually connected the dots between the house and the grocery store, the lake with a hiking trail, the few other places I knew to look for here in Nashville, the town in which I had been born but where I had not lived since I was a toddler, a place 250 miles from the city where my house, my spouse, my children, my obligations and responsibilities, were rooted.

It felt like fate that I'd ended up here. A few weeks after the conversation about how to live von Furstenberg style, I had come up with another idea—a version of "away" that made a bit more sense. I floated the idea past John over dinner one night: "What if I went somewhere by myself, just temporarily, while the kids are at camp this summer? Somewhere I could, I don't know, rest my brain." That, we could figure out.

It was only days later that I heard from one of my best friends, who lives in Nashville. She told me about her friend, who was in a tough spot. Her friend, like me, needed some time away. She'd been through a divorce, the deaths of both her parents, and a hell year at work. Her boss was insisting she take advantage of her backlogged vacation time, and she'd found a place to stay at the beach for a few weeks, but she couldn't take the cat, and she didn't have the funds to afford a house sitter or boarding fees.

That's how I ended up with a free place to stay and a job feeding a cat named Winston.

In the journal I kept during those weeks, Winston makes frequent appearances.

DAY 3: *Winston walked into kitchen when I started the can opener. Ate his food and ran back out.*

DAY 4: *Who came up with the concept of a litter box? Why did other people adopt it? Why didn't everyone look at that person and say, "That's a terrible idea, Mike"?*

DAY 6: *I am on the sofa and Winston is on the floor and he's staring at me. I just thought,* My cat is trying to tell me something, *and at first I freaked out because I didn't*

*know how I'd figure out what he's trying to say. But this
is not my cat! I don't need to learn his language. We can
exist here for a little while without understanding each other.
Everything in his house will go back to normal soon. This is
just a pause. I just said "pause" out loud to the cat. What
if he thinks I said "paws"?*

Other prevalent themes in my journal included my daily physical activity ("Hiked around Radnor Lake for 30 minutes") and
errands ("Found my way to Walgreens and got paper towels").
I was very good at recording my comings and goings, which
were few.

I wasn't entirely alone during my alone time. My old friend
lived nearby in the same part of Nashville, and she came over
a couple of times a week for coffee. I was acquainted with a
few of her book club buddies, who welcomed me as well. I
enjoyed the occasional lunch or dinner with these people, but
mostly I went on walks by myself or stayed in the little house,
with the invisible cat, moving from chair to sofa to deck steps
to chair. I did enough editing work to keep my clients satisfied,
sending someone a document or two every few days; but as
usual for the summer, the workload was light. I didn't need to
check email very often.

It was a vacation of sorts from my regular life. But one of
the reasons I kept to myself so much was that I didn't want it
to feel too much like a vacation. I wasn't there to have a good
time and paint the town. I was there to experience aloneness,
to see if getting what I needed would make me feel better.
Sometimes a change of scenery had helped me see myself as

a new character; sometimes it hadn't. I didn't know whether this time would work, whether fresh surroundings would help me reset my mental health.

I talked to John once a day by phone. "What are you thinking about?" he'd ask.

"Nothing," I'd say. I wasn't deflecting. It wasn't like when you ask your child what they did at school and they say "Nothing," even though they did a lot of somethings. I was truly focused on having as little as possible to think about. I was tired of thinking. I wanted to purge the running commentary inside my own head: *You are broken. Something is wrong with you. You can't succeed at the life you are living. WHAT ARE YOU GOING TO DO?*

Later, I would realize that I had been doing a lot of meditating, although I didn't fully understand what meditating was at the time and wouldn't have called it that. I just knew that whenever a thought entered my head, I ushered it back out, protecting the emptiness. I craved nothingness—no agenda, no chatter. Just blessed silence.

I used to make fun of women who ran off to yoga retreats to find themselves. Not being a yoga person myself, I didn't get it. I didn't understand why stretching was somehow a transformative experience. (I'm sorry, I know there is so much more to yoga than stretching, but that's what it looks like to me.) I once joked to a friend that Lululemon should come out with a line of midlife-crisis pants and finding-yourself bras. They'd sell like crazy.

But I get it now. It must be the meditative aspect of yoga that makes it such a draw for people whose minds are crowded with anxious voices. It must be the stillness. The permission to disengage.

I wanted to be quiet and small.

DAY 9: *Found a recipe card in a kitchen drawer for "hot buttered crackers," which calls for tossing saltines in butter and dry salad dressing mix and putting them under the broiler. Why does this require a recipe? Is it gross?*

DAY 11: *Winston sat in a chair next to my chair while I drank tea. Maybe in cat-world, we are friends now. Made hot buttered crackers.*

DAY 12: *Hot buttered crackers should be called hot buttered crack.*

Mostly, when I felt the need to engage with something, I read. I'd packed a box of books I'd gotten behind on—novels I'd bought but never started, self-help books with inspirational titles like *Daring Greatly*, books about business and technology and science and nature and all sorts of things I wondered about and felt the need to have answers to. Because I was doing so little else, I ran through the books more quickly than I'd expected.

Lucky for me, my friend worked in the local bookstore. "Come with me to work," she said. "You can find something new."

I knew about Parnassus Books already, of course. It was owned by the writer Ann Patchett and her business partner,

Karen Hayes. I'd read about it on the front page of the *New York Times* after it opened: "Novelist Fights the Tide by Opening a Bookstore." The store had a certain kind of fame among book lovers. I was excited to visit.

What a jewel of a place. *Store* feels like too commercial and impersonal a word. This was not a store like Target or Kroger or the place where you get car batteries. This was a home. Books nestled together in tidy lines along every wall, bunked up on wooden shelves under warm yellow lights. Booksellers milled about, each busily tending to some task or another: climbing a ladder to pull down a memoir, shelving a stack of paperbacks, tying ribbons around gift-wrapped bundles at the register. Customers—but again, the word feels too impersonal; they seemed like they must all be neighbors or cousins—treated each other like friends, or at least acquaintances, passing books back and forth over the New Fiction table. I stayed for about an hour, imagining I shopped there all the time, too; then I bought a few novels and took them back to the house.

I went back a couple of days later. And again a couple of days after that.

One afternoon, I wandered back to the office at the far end of the store and said hello to the three women seated there, each of them barely visible behind stacks of paperbacks heaped on their desks, a busy, joyful mess. They waved cheerfully and asked what I was reading. I wanted to stretch my arms against the store's wall and hug it.

DAY 15: *Figured out how to stream TV on the laptop. Watched six episodes of* The Good Wife, *season one.*

*When the show comes on and the house fills with strangers'*
*voices, Winston goes back under the bed.*

One afternoon my friend came over and asked for my help writing an email. She wanted to ask her boss at the bookstore for a raise and a promotion. "I've been subbing for someone on the late shift and I like it," she said. "I think I should be the assistant manager and always work evenings."

"But what about when school starts back up?" I asked. Her son was the same age as mine and in middle school, which meant lots of homework. I hated homework more than anything. It made my already exhausted children desperately frustrated and turned what could have been relaxing family time at the end of the day into teeth-gnashing, paper-crumpling torture sessions. When John was home, it was bad enough; but if he was working late or traveling, the lack of his patient presence made everything worse. I tried to give pep talks—"Check your work! Write neatly! Stop fiddling with your eraser!"—but my attempts to help only stressed the kids out more. We were often war-torn and raw by the time bedtime rolled around. I figured it was like this for everyone.

"Oh, I'm terrible at homework time," my friend said. "I'm better at handling the mornings, so my husband and I split it up. He leaves for work early and I stay at work late. He handles dinnertime and I do breakfast."

It may seem crazy, but that conversation was a revelation for me.

My friend explained it all so calmly: She hated homework, so she got a job at homework time and handed homework over to her husband. She and her family had all made an adjustment in their lives in order for things to be better for everyone. She didn't look at her new routine like a failure to make her old routine work; she looked at it like a sensible solution. No big deal.

*You can just change things*, I thought. What a concept.

DAY 18: *Watched six more episodes of* The Good Wife. *If I had a cat, I would name it Alicia Florrick.*

DAY 19: *Made it to season three of* The Good Wife. *Donuts for dinner for me. A can of Poultry-Lovers Dinner for Winston. He's a poultry lover.*

I fed the cat. I watered the plants. I watched my show about a woman taking control of her life. I walked. I read. I slept. I sat. I felt like a fist unclenching. I could remember, with greater clarity than I had in years, the person I was before I was a speck on a highway clogged with other specks.

Sensory memories came dislodged and bubbled up to my mind's surface: A shadow fell over the chair where I sat staring out the window at a spider, and I remembered the fuzzy webs among the old shoes at the back of my childhood closet, where I sat sometimes to read. I tied my sneakers to go for a walk, and I could smell the asphalt track where I walked with my friends at lunchtime in middle school. I bent to pick a fallen twig out of the monkey grass along the back deck, and suddenly I was running my fingertip along the notched edge of a leaf on my mother's rosebushes. It was as if, given the quiet and permission to come out, past iterations of myself were emerging from their places in my memory and tumbling one over another, allowing me to sort through them and remember who I'd been. Who I still was.

We coexisted in that house for those weeks, all the me's.

I had phone calls with my therapist once a week.

"Sometimes I drive around Nashville and don't even go anywhere," I told her once.

"What goes through your mind as you drive?" she asked.

"It's so green," I said. "They say the traffic's bad here, but it's nothing like Atlanta. It doesn't feel like the city is screaming all the time."

"What do you think about when you think of going home?"

"I think, 'Maybe I can try to feel like this there.'"

"Do you think you can?"

"I don't know," I said.

DAY 20: *I am too smart to go back to being miserable.*

# Ungrateful Bitch

I know how fortunate I am to have my health and my family and my jobs and my roof and my car and my democracy. I do know. I promise. And I know that saying out loud, "I think I might want a different life," when you already have a perfectly good life is sort of like holding a half-eaten chocolate chip cookie in your hand while saying, "I don't want a chocolate chip cookie. I think I want some other kind of cookie." I know some people have no cookies.

Unfortunately, having a fine life doesn't exempt anyone from existential angst. Maybe it should. Maybe if we were all perfect people, we'd wake up in our nice warm beds, appreciate that we're not waking up on concrete under an overpass, and cease fretting about our hopes and dreams, because if our basic biological needs are covered—food, shelter, water—what else could be so bad? Perhaps if I were homeless, I wouldn't give a damn about things like professional satisfaction or personal fulfillment, because my greater concern would be not freezing to death. But I know damn well that once I had food in my belly and a roof over my head, I'd start thinking about those things again. The horizon of needs and wants never actually gets closer; it's an illusion, a trick. We can always want more. We can always perceive some need.

Robert Browning wrote, "Ah, but a man's reach should exceed his grasp, / Or what's a heaven for?" and I feel him on that. But I also say, Okay Bob, what about a woman's reach? You could fill a canyon with all that's been written about women wanting "it all" and whether "it all" is fair to want and what the hell even *is* "it all" and how tired we all are of the backlash against backlash against backlash against that whole overplayed conversation. But I think the question people are arguing about when they fight about it isn't *What should women want?* but *Should women want?* I mean, hey, America gave us the right to vote. We've got some high-powered lady-CEO role models now. There are breastfeeding lounges in airports. We have so much! Shouldn't we stop all this unseemly wanting? Of course not. I know that's bullshit, even as I know I still feel a little guilty whenever I want more or different than I have.

Knowing all this doesn't change anything.

Remember that little mermaid? You might say she got what was coming to her for reaching too far, but I understand how she felt. She had a good life underwater, but she wanted a different one on land. Is that so terrible?

I get the guilt thing. I imagine, sometimes, that when I stick up for what I need or insist on what I want, people are whispering behind my back, calling me an ungrateful bitch. They're not. (At least I don't think so.) That voice is coming from inside me. I have to talk myself out of it. I have to remind myself that wanting doesn't make anyone an ungrateful bitch.

Or maybe it does.

Does it matter?

I mean, think about it—if you *are* an ungrateful bitch, then you're an ungrateful bitch whether somebody else thinks you are or not. The ship of bitchy ingratitude has sailed, so why not climb on board and sail it somewhere interesting? Either I'm an ungrateful bitch or I'm not, but I've decided I don't care which.

I made up a helpful exercise for whenever I'm worried about doing something that I believe, deep down, is important and necessary because I'm afraid someone might call me an ungrateful bitch. I'll share it here in case anyone else needs to try it. It goes like this:

March over to the nearest mirror. Put your hands on your hips, look yourself right in the eye and say, "You ungrateful bitch."

Walk outside to get the mail. When a car drives by, mouth the words *UN-GRATE-FUL BIIIITCH* at the driver while hooking both thumbs at yourself, so they know.

Stop to look at an earthworm. Crouch low and look the little guy in the face—or the ass, it's hard to tell on a worm—and say, "You know what I am, little fella? I'm an ungrateful bitch."

Now, go to a coffee shop. When they ask what name to put on your cup, spell it out: U-N-G-R-A-T-E-F-U-L B-I-T-C-H.

Change your phone greeting to, "You have reached an ungrateful bitch, leave a message."

Write the words down—*ungrateful bitch*—and stare at them until they're just squiggles and shapes.

Say it out loud until the syllables are no more than the clatter of forks and knives in a drawer, the whir of an engine, the shushing slide of pages as you thumb a stack of blank paper. White noise.

*Ungrateful bitch.*
*Ungrateful bitch?*
*Ungrateful bitch!*

# Sloths on a Waterbed

**My** friend Corrine couldn't wait to move into her new condo. The trouble was what to do with the spare room.

We were in our early thirties. Corrine was newly single, and she'd already set up the master bedroom as hers. She could do anything she wanted with the second bedroom, but she was hung up on the idea that she was supposed to have a guest room.

"I want to put a desk in there and build some shelves," she said. She wanted to be able to leave work earlier on weeknights and stop going to her office on weekends. Plus she'd been bookmarking chic home-office designs for years.

"Do it," I said. "Build your room."

"But then where would I put a guest bed?"

I asked if she anticipated having a lot of guests. She said no, out-of-towners almost never came to visit. But doesn't everyone have a guest room? Isn't that what homeowners do? And what if she did have guests one day?

"Look at it like this," I said. "Are you willing to live without your dream office—which you know you'd use every day— just so you can have a guest room sitting there unused most of the time?"

She built the office. If a guest decided to come through town, she could blow up a mattress or get them a hotel room. Arrangements could always be made.

I've come back to that conversation again and again.

I thought about it when John and I started playing with the idea of moving to Tennessee.

Nashville hadn't cured me. It didn't change me into someone else. But it did help me see myself and my life in a new way. It helped me remember what it felt like to be me, just *me*, not lonely-and-traffic-crazed-me. It reminded me that I could change things about my daily existence to make it fit me better, which made me ponder whether there might be a daily existence that fit our whole family better.

Shortly after my summer in Nashville, I got a call from the bookstore. They were looking to do some marketing projects, maybe start an online magazine. They offered me a job, the deal being that I'd do the bulk of the work from afar, commuting up to Tennessee a couple of times a month for meetings or events.

Being in Nashville again on a semi-regular basis improved my mental state considerably. I loved the way I spent my days there. I'd go into the store for a few hours, then have lunch or dinner with a friend or colleague, maybe go hear some music, and do some quiet reading and writing. The city was full of literary and creative types, culturally curious people who shared my passions. The parents of kids my kids' ages were as likely to be novelists, actors, or drummers as doctors, lawyers, or accountants.

The Jason Isbell song "Alabama Pines" was playing on the radio a lot then, and I always teared up at the line "No one gives a damn about the things I give a damn about." In Atlanta, I once scored a last-minute pair of tickets to a midnight Brandi Carlile concert at a bar, lucking into a truly rare opportunity to see my musical hero in a small venue. John was out of town, and I called at least ten friends, but no one wanted to go. I ended up going by myself and sitting among strangers. In Nashville, people gave a damn about the things I gave a damn about.

Of course, in Nashville I was free of most of the pressures and hassles of everyday life I had back in Atlanta. I didn't have a house to take care of because I was always staying at a friend's place (some people do need guest rooms!). I didn't have to make dinner for anyone but myself; I wasn't needed at any school events; the mundanities of active parenthood were not part of my life there. I missed my family when I was in Nashville, though. I wanted to sit down with John at the end of the day and talk. I wanted to take the kids with me to see and do all the city had to offer. Nashville's biggest downside was that my three best people weren't there. But instead of thinking, *I should go home to them*, I thought, *I should bring them here*.

Part of me felt like I couldn't leave Atlanta because we were rooted there. That's where so many of our friends lived, and I loved my friends. But the truth was that I hardly saw them. Atlanta was like Corinne's guest room—a space I was holding on to just in case it might get used for a certain purpose that, in fact, it was almost never used for. Corinne didn't have guests 99 percent of the time, and 99 percent of the time my Atlanta friends were too busy with their own growing families and commitments to hang out.

Then there were the practical considerations: The traffic in Nashville was nothing compared to Atlanta. You could zip from one place to another in fifteen minutes. The houses cost less. The schools were just as good as the ones in Atlanta.

We decided to go. John started looking for a job, and I started looking for a place for us to live. I swore to all my friends that the minute they wanted to do something fun—go on a trip, throw a birthday party, see a show—I'd hop in the car and be there in less than four hours. But spending day after day sitting in Atlanta waiting for that life to turn into something it wasn't didn't make sense anymore. There was no alternate life taking place in another universe. There was no time machine. We had just this one timeline, and it was ticking forward.

I guess it's crazy that I thought people would embrace our choice, but it had been such a hard decision, and I was proud of it. It had taken so long for me to accept that two things I believed—"I love my friends here so much" and "I don't want to live here anymore"—could coexist. To reconcile two contradictory ideas, you have to find a way for one of them to win out, to subjugate one to the other. It drove me nuts that I couldn't do that with this decision. I loved my Atlanta people *and* I wanted to leave Atlanta. Both. To make a decision, I had to acknowledge that neither was more true than the other and that my way forward wouldn't negate either truth. I could love my friends even as I made my decision to go.

After wrestling through this dilemma, I wanted everyone to share my pride in it. Talk about naive . . . Telling people we were leaving was one of the hardest things about moving. I wanted to say, "I'm doing something you're not going to like, but I love you, and it's important to me that you cheer me on as I do it, if you possibly can." I never verbalized that, though. Instead, I blurted it out.

"So, we're going to do it. We're going to take a trip up there and look for a house," I told a dear friend.

"Couldn't you just join a tennis team?" she asked, half joking.

My friend knew I needed a fresh start; she just wished it could be of a different kind. She knew I'd found something in Nashville life that I didn't have in Atlanta. "I'm going away" is difficult for people to hear, because it sounds like "I'm going away from you." It's hard to sound happy for someone who is leaving you. When a beloved bookseller quit working at the store recently to go to grad school, we presented her with a cake that read FUCK YOU, LINDSAY in icing. Back when I worked in consulting, I once said "No!" to a coworker when she told me she was having a baby. I didn't mean, "Oh no, your baby is terrible." I meant, "Oh no, we won't get to go to happy hour after work anymore."

People said other things, too.

"How could you do this to your kids?"

I got that one a couple of times, and it hit me in the gut. Of course I worried about how the move would affect our children. If all those moves during my own childhood had turned me into someone who needed a fresh start every few years, would moving my children now do the same thing to them? Would

217

they ever forgive us for taking them away from their childhood home and friends?

Then again, I reminded myself, all we were doing was moving. It's not that big a deal. We weren't sending our kids to go live on the moon. We were going, all together, three and a half hours up the road to a perfectly civilized place—a wonderful place, really—where the children would be fed and clothed and educated, just as they always had been. They'd have to adjust to some change, yes. But they might even like Nashville better.

And one move during childhood—especially in the age of the internet, where it's infinitely easier to keep up with people—probably wouldn't have the same effect as half a dozen moves, would it?

We also heard: "Ugh."

It's impossible to spell the actual sound I mean here—it's more guttural than "ugh," sort of a combination of "unh" and "yecch"—but you'd know it if you heard it. It's hardly more than a forceful exhale, really. A verbal eye roll. It conveys sentiments like, "Oh come on, that's stupid," or, "Who do you think you are?" It's dismissive, but there's also an undertone of bitterness to it.

I understand this one, too. Social scientists call it "crab mentality." Say there are a bunch of crabs at the bottom of a bucket, and one crab starts trying to crawl out. Instead of giving that crab a boost, the others grab at him with their pincers, pulling him back into the bucket. If they're going to be in the bucket, they want everyone to be in the bucket.

I'd change the crabs-in-a-bucket analogy to make it a bit gentler, though. Some of the people who looked askance at our plans were dear to us. I can't think of them as crabs. They were surprised and perhaps hurt and, maybe some of them, a little unsure about their own choices. It's that confirmation bias thing again: People want to believe the choices they've made about where and how they live are right, and sometimes the easiest way to do that is by deciding that all other choices are wrong. If we were choosing to leave life in Atlanta behind, did that mean we thought everyone who stayed was making the wrong choice? No, but it's typical for the human brain to react that way. So I've got to go with some analogy that's a little more endearing than crabs. Let's say sloths. I love sloths.

Sloths are slow-moving. Inertia is their jam. Often, in a tight group of human friends, an unspoken accord congeals over time, an agreement that not only are we all in this life together, but we must also *do* everything together. It can make a reasonable move look radical simply because it veers away from the group.

I'd amend the bucket part of the analogy, too. Our life in Atlanta wasn't a bucket. We weren't trapped. I *felt* trapped, but that was a function of my own mind—the way you can feel claustrophobic sitting in a wide-open room if you don't want to be in it. I no longer wanted to be there. But I wasn't being held anywhere against my will, and it was no less objectively lovely a place just because I wanted out. So let's not say the sloths are in a bucket. Let's say they're on a waterbed. A big, comfortable waterbed that's easy to sink into and hard to get up from. I remember climbing onto my friend Jen's mom's waterbed when we were ten years old. When we were ready to climb off, we couldn't steady our hands and knees, and the waves rolling within the mattress kept knocking us back down. We snorted and giggled, but there was panic in our laughter, too.

I told myself my friendships were like snuggly sloths on a waterbed, and I was the weird sloth who wanted off, and all of this was normal.

It's not easy to be a people-pleaser who chooses to do something that doesn't please people, especially if you've got that little kid inside your head wanting to be praised and told she's the best. But sometimes you have to do the thing you have to do, even if it makes people mad. Even if it makes you feel like you've lost the support of people you want in your corner. Even if it feels like some people are giving you a big fat F instead of an A+.

There was one other thing people said a lot: "How'd you do it?"

John heard this less than I did, but I heard it many, many times. Always in hushed tones, in conversations that began with someone pulling me aside—like they were about to ask me for the number of my weed dealer. These friends and acquaintances were the ones who got giddy when they found out what we were doing. "I've been thinking about moving to _____ for years!" they'd say. Or, "We talk about it all the time. How'd you finally decide to go?" And, "Was it hard to sell your house?" As it turns out, change appeals to lots of people. "Tell me," they'd ask, "do you think I could do it, too?"

"Build your room," I always said.

# And Then the Dog Died

In moving, as in life, there are so many things you think you can control and so few that you actually can.

This is how I envisioned our family's final night as Atlanta residents: We'd eat at our favorite pizza place, sit out on our back porch until dark, and then drift off to sleep in our rooms one last time.

This is what actually happened: Just before dinner on that muggy June evening, Eleanor Roosevelt, the younger of our two beagles, suffered the rupture of an infected anal gland, requiring John to pack her off to the emergency vet while I stayed home with both children and our other hound, Phoebe, while fielding questions such as, "Can a dog die of an exploded butt?" Our night was shot, to the tune of $350 and a shaved dog-bottom. Eleanor was just fine when she and John finally got home around midnight, but our picture-perfect sunset farewell to our city did not happen. We followed the moving truck over the Georgia-Tennessee border the next day a little more frazzled than we'd intended to be, Eleanor Roosevelt banging her plastic cone against the back of my seat the whole way, and her big sister, Phoebe, growling her displeasure with the noise. None of this was quite as we'd expected.

One night several months earlier, John whispered from the pillow next to me, "But where will we be buried?"

Moving meant sorting through lots of questions, like, did we want a house or a condo? Would we live in town or out in the country? And—if you're John and this is how your mind works, I guess—where should our earthly remains be placed if we were to die in our new city?

"Wait, you want to be buried?" I said. "I thought you wanted to be cremated."

"I don't know, now we're going to Nashville—maybe there's somewhere there I'd rather be."

"Technically, you wouldn't *rather* anything. You'd be dead."

"But where would my friends go for my funeral?"

We stayed on this topic for several minutes before I started getting frustrated.

"Do we have to know where our bodies will go after we die to know where we want to live right now?" I asked.

If figuring out what step to take next meant we immediately had to figure out every step afterward, too, then taking the next step would be impossible. I was tired of needing to know all the answers. I wanted *just enough* answers. (Also, I truly do not care what anybody does with my body after I'm dead. Dress it up in a sequined jumpsuit and fly it from a flagpole if you want. I won't need it anymore.)

"Let's look at life in chunks," I said. "Right now, we just

need to answer the questions relevant to this next chunk. When we get to that chunk, we'll figure out the chunk after that."

"Okay, fine," John said. "Chunks."

Then we spent ten minutes giggling over the word *chunks*, which sounds really funny when you whisper it repeatedly.

Breaking the news to the kids that our family would be moving away from the only place they'd ever called home gave me a new respect for my mother and all the times she had to do the same thing for me.

When we first had even the tiniest inkling that a move might be a possibility, I started taking our kids with me on jaunts to Nashville—a day here, an overnight there. They got to hang out at the bookstore and read all the free books they could fit into their heads while I was in meetings with authors and booksellers. In the afternoons, I handed them each a dollar and sent them down the sidewalk to Fox's Donut Den. By the time the move had begun to look like a reality, we had successfully brainwashed them enough that when I casually mentioned, "We're going to try living in Nashville for a while," my son responded, "Nashville? I love Nashville!"

"Books and donuts!" my daughter said.

Telling them was easier than I'd thought, but it didn't quell my uncertainty as I thought it might. I often had days that spring when I thought, *What the hell are we doing?* I told myself that if it didn't work out, we could always move back.

I held on to that thought as I watched hulking men in matching blue shirts wrap protective plastic around our kitchen table, our sofa, and our mattresses and load them into the moving truck. Part of my brain wanted to be absolutely positive we were doing the right thing; the other part knew there was no way to be sure about anything.

I read somewhere that children need to know they can rely on some things to stay the same, even when a big transition comes along. So I put a lot of thought into creating a sense of consistency in order to manage how much change and disorder our kids would experience. Now, of course, I can see that this concept makes as much sense as a "birth plan."

We timed everything to happen over the summer. We thought it would be easier to handle the move-related chaos in a season when everything's a little more laid-back. Can't find the box with sheets and pillows in it? That's okay, there's no rush on bedtime. Don't have an oven in the kitchen yet? No problem. Throw something on the grill and eat outside. Summer was indeed a perfect time to explore our new surroundings. We could go for a hike on a weekday morning, lie around reading in the afternoon. We went to concerts, parks, and movies, and tried all our neighborhood sandwich shops and ice cream parlors. (I put on a dozen pounds in our first year there. That's what happens when you grab hold of your city with both hands and stuff it in your face.)

For a couple of early months, Nashville was one big vacation. And for those two months, not once did either of the children say they missed Atlanta. The chaos seemed under control. Yes, we were in a new place. And yes, we'd begun renovations on our house right after we moved into it. Sometimes we woke up at 6:30 a.m. to the sound of buzz saws in our kitchen. But I made sure to keep a lot of things the same: same morning schedule of walking our dogs and making beds. Same routines and rules. The locale may have been new, but that didn't mean everything else had to change, too.

Then, as summer got shorter and shorter, reality began to kick in.

My children, like most, have never been wild about getting pulled out of bed before they're fully awake. They have never liked having to stop playing to take a shower or brush their teeth. They've always dragged their feet when it's time to put on shoes or jackets or whatever else prevents them from running free and barefoot and barely clothed through the world the way they want to. The annual letdown of returning to the weekday grind had everyone at our house a little on edge. The more stressed they felt, the more they desired the familiar and the old. Without those comforts to soothe their anxiety, their stress came out in uncharacteristic outbursts over small things. Suddenly old complaints had a recurrent new theme.

When I told my son to put on a raincoat, he cursed Nashville's weather: "The sun NEVER comes out!"

When I asked my daughter to pick up the piles of Legos in the hall, she broke down: "I don't even know WHERE LEGOS GO HERE."

They came to experience what we adults already know: When you move, you take more than just your stuff with you. You take yourself. You take all your likes, dislikes, hangups, hopes, and problems, and you place them in a new and unfamiliar setting. Certain things are true no matter where you are. If you're a kid, the end of summer blows, wherever you live.

Still, we had it all under control.

Then both children got pink eye and ear infections and nasty colds.

And a toilet broke.

And a car battery gave out.

And we busted a batch of carpenter ants living in our shower.

And just to keep things exciting, a family of mice took up residence in the garage.

And then sweet old Phoebe—the beagle who had been with us for fourteen years and served as a surrogate parent to pup Eleanor Roosevelt—left us. She was sleeping in a kennel at the veterinary clinic, boarding while we were out of town overnight, when she died. Our vet called to deliver the news, "I'm afraid Phoebe didn't wake up this morning."

"Okay," I said. "Okay." *Okay, okay, okay*, I mouthed to myself as I hung up the phone.

Telling the children about their dog was so much harder than telling them we were moving.

Much sobbing ensued.

When I went in to pick up Eleanor Roosevelt from the kennel that afternoon, I made a joke about whether I'd still have to pay for both dogs considering I'd dropped off two and was getting only one back. The front-desk staff laughed the kind of nervous chuckle you do when you're afraid of upsetting a crazy person.

A few days after we lost Phoebe, on a hectic Monday morning, I was trying to hustle the children to the car to go meet their new pediatrician, so we could have the health forms completed for their new school. I couldn't find my keys, it was ninety-five degrees out, and I was also wrestling a basket of laundry out the front door to drop at the laundromat, because the washer and dryer were a week late being installed. Everyone was sweating and fussing at one another.

I put Eleanor Roosevelt into the bathroom she and Phoebe had been sharing as a makeshift dog room during the construction. "You take a nap," I said. "We'll be back soon."

She started howling. And howling and howling. The saddest little I've-never-been-an-only-dog-before-please-don't-leave-me howl.

The pitiful howling kept up for days. Exercise, playtime, a new bone—nothing helped. She moped around the house and yard. When I was at home writing, she sat under my chair. When I left the room, she followed me. If she couldn't go with me, she bayed at the door. She was heartbroken.

"Mom," my son said, "Eleanor Roosevelt is lonely. Are we going to get another dog?"

Was it part of our plan to adopt a new dog the week before

starting school in a new city, while our house was still half under construction? Oh, hell no. But we're a two-dog family, and we were one dog down. This was no time for the plan.

So the next day, we headed off to the Love at First Sight shelter. There we met a yellow pup, some kind of Labrador mix brought in with an abandoned litter. He had just started eating (and eating and eating) again after recovering from a nearly fatal bout of parvovirus, and his kibble-filled belly ballooned out on either side of his scrawny ribs. This little fellow was the last boy pup of his siblings left—the others, all prettier and pudgier, had been adopted.

I bet he didn't think his summer was going to go like this either.

He rolled around with the other shelter puppies on the floor. When I crouched down, he skidded and skated across the linoleum and burrowed between my knees, tail a-wagging. Contrary to plan but consistent with everyone's desires, I looked up at the vet tech and said, "This one." I couldn't believe what I was doing, but I also couldn't wait to tell John we'd found the exact dog he'd been wanting all his life.

"Remember how you said that one day when you had a real yard, you'd want a big dog, like a yellow Lab?" I asked him that afternoon. "Guess what? I found your yellow Lab puppy."

"At last—my big dog!" John said.

We all laughed and decided to call the new pup Woodstock, a beagle's best friend.

Sure enough, Woodstock and John bonded fast. Woodstock let John feed him his mushy vet-approved food from a spoon. Woodstock ran to the front door every evening when he heard John's car arrive. And as days passed, Woodstock grew . . .

kind of. His body got longer and longer, and his legs stayed more or less the same. "What a funny little Lab he is," we'd say, wondering when his height would catch up with his length.

At his six-month checkup, we asked the vet what she guessed his heritage was. Lab-hound? Lab-shepherd?

"This dog? Oh, he's some kind of dachshund mix, maybe a little terrier or something," she said.

Of course he was.

# Wish List

**Every** December, we go through this. It's like someone hits the "play" button on a favorite holiday song, and we all remember the words we've sung countless times.

Here we are again: When I sense it coming, I begin burying my phone at the bottom of my purse with the sound turned off. I'm trying to ignore the calls, emails, and texts from well-meaning relatives, all of whom are asking, *Where is the Christmas list?*

They want suggestions for what to give the kids, the more specific the better. If I say, "Maybe a book?" they'll ask, "Which one?"

I don't know which one. I still haven't given much thought to holiday shopping. I despise the charmless online gift registry, it's true, but my reluctance to create—on command—a catalog of child-appropriate gifts is more than just resistance to materialism.

I think it's about longing: to be taken care of, to let someone else do at least part of the planning. I may be an adult, but some part of me still has a child's desire to wake up, starry-eyed, and find that gifts have materialized by some kind of magic under the tree—surprises chosen with love and obtained in secret, waiting to be opened in wonder. We don't outgrow that. On some level, we are all still five-year-olds.

Then there's the guilt, of course. I suspect our relatives wouldn't need ideas for what to give our children if I did a better job of keeping in touch during the rest of the year. If we visited more often—if I were a better daughter and sister—they'd know all my kids' hobbies and wishes, and I would know theirs. (I haven't asked anyone for a Christmas list in several years. I hope the recipients don't hate their gifts from me, but I really do enjoy putting a little imagination into them.)

This is also a practical matter. To compile an itemized inventory of wished-for things and divvy it up among grandparents and aunts and uncles would require time, of which I have no surplus. Tonight, for example, I have four events to attend—two optional-but-encouraged work functions, a fundraiser for my children's school, and an already rescheduled social gathering. I don't know if our son's soccer game will finish in time for the first event or at what point in the evening my husband's meeting will let out so that he can come home to watch our daughter.

I don't know what anyone's going to eat for dinner or when, much less what everyone's getting for Christmas.

Maybe I'm having a misplaced and cranky response to the rise of entitlement culture. There's a transactional aspect to giving now, a way of forcing a script onto what used to be spontaneous. This has trickled down from wedding and baby gift registries to birthdays and holidays, not only for adults but for children, too. Online personal registry services have evolved to serve the demand. Apps let you tag items you want, right down to preferred color and size. God forbid someone show you generosity you didn't explicitly request.

Where's the line between writing a letter to the North Pole and forking over an itemized file of material desires? The former seems sweet; the latter feels like handing someone a grocery list. Plus, if you ask only for things you know exist, how will you ever be delighted by something you couldn't have anticipated?

The emphasis on the things themselves suggests that the holiday's success or failure—as if a holiday could *be* a success or a failure—hinges on the rightness of the gifts. In fact, that's what retailers would have us believe. Before the last gingerbread crumbs have been swallowed, the post-holiday sales pipe up, "Didn't get what you really wanted? Let's fix that."

Still, it's my job as a parent to orchestrate all the steps that make Christmas look like magic, and that means I have to make the decisions. We're lucky to have family who love our kids, who want to do something nice for them, and I know it's unkind not to return their calls. I may be an ungrateful bitch sometimes, but I know better than to blow off a grandmother who loves her grandchildren. So I dig the phone out of my purse.

"Anything is fine, really," I try to tell my mother-in-law. I tell my own mom, "They like everything. Maybe clothes?"

"That doesn't help me," my mom says.

That's when I realize she and I are experiencing variations of the same feeling: *Help me. Make this easier, please. Tell me what to do.*

At the end of the school day, my daughter climbs into the car. Thanks to her brother's sports schedule, she has done her homework on bleachers and in backseats for three of the past four nights. "What's for dinner?" she asks.

"I'm not sure yet," I say. "What are you in the mood for?"

"Whatever," she says. "You pick."

She wants me to decide. I want someone else to decide. My mother wants me to decide. We don't grow out of this either, apparently. It's funny how the same conversation happens every year, with the same undertones: *You* make all the decisions. No, *you* make all the decisions. I guess this means there is no age when we stop wishing to be taken care of. Good to know.

I make a decision: No events tonight. Not one, not two, not three, not four. I make the calls and beg off. "I'm sorry. I wish I could come." And it's true; I wish I could be many places at once. But I can't.

We go to the soccer game. We come home. I make spaghetti. John and our son hang out after homework and talk about whether the deer in our yard have enough to eat when it turns cold. My daughter and I share a blanket on the sofa. She's braiding the fringe when I ask, "If Mimi"—her grandmother, my mother—"wanted to give you something you really liked for Christmas, do you have any ideas for her?" She looks up and ponders for a moment, then says, "Maybe a few yards of fabric? I want to make a cape." I reach for paper and pen, start making a list. That wasn't so hard. "What else?" I ask.

So I make the list this year. I will do it every year, after I resist for a little while and then give up resisting, after I remember that I have been that daughter, I will be that grandmother.

# The Unaccountable
# Weight of Accountability

I stood in the middle of a forest and silent-screamed every profane word I know, which is a lot of bad words.

For the second time in one morning, I was on a wooded park trail. The first time, I'd decided to cram in a mini-hike before doing an hour of writing and then heading to a meeting for work. Then I got home, checked my pockets, and found that my driver's license had gone missing. So back I went, hiking the same route a second time, eyes scanning the ground for my lost card. An hour later, there I was under the trees, still no license, my precious hour of writing time gone. *This is what I get for trying to exercise*, I thought. Later, I ate a packet of gummy fruit snacks in my car on the way to my meeting.

I reported this episode to my various accountability groups—sets of friends who'd decided to check in on a daily or weekly basis to hold each other's feet to the fire of various goals. There's the fitness group; I'm supposed to check in with them weekly about how many days I've worked out. There's the healthy-eating group, in which we keep a text thread circulating to log accomplishments such as, "Drank green juice instead of Diet Coke." Then there's the writing group, five

237

nonfiction writers who also have day jobs. We meet weekly before work and use a private Facebook page to hold each other to our pledge not to let our creative endeavors get pushed aside by workaday tasks.

In Dani Shapiro's memoir *Hourglass*, she quotes something the writer Grace Paley once said: The years between ages fifty and eighty go by so fast they feel less like minutes, more like seconds. I suspect Paley and Shapiro are right, although I'm not there yet, so I can't say for sure. What I can say is that my early forties are ticking by at an alarming rate. The idea of making my days count makes me feel like I'm not wasting them.

Accountability is all the rage, and not just in our own lives. Whenever something bad happens, people insist on finding someone to hold accountable—as if that will undo anything. It's a buzzword in the business and political worlds, code for "responsibility" and "the buck stops here." Being accountable means you reply promptly to emails at work, you finish what you start, and you spend money wisely. It means every move you make counts toward something. The higher up the ranks you go, the greater accountability you have on your shoulders.

Personally, I'm glad I'm not an elected official or a CEO, because I can't take any more accountability. The more people and forces I have to answer to, the more "held accountable" starts to feel like "held underwater." Some days, I want to spend an afternoon online looking at pictures of dogs with eyebrows, and I don't want to have to report it to anyone. Some nights, I want to spend $9.99 to buy a movie on-demand even though I could wait a week and rent it for $2.99, and I want to revel in that foolish splurge by myself.

As it is, I find I can only clear the bar for one accountability group at a time. As an approval-seeking person, I always want a gold star. But to achieve one thing generally means letting go of another. I can write, but only—as they say—by putting my butt in the chair. If my butt is in the chair, my butt is not outside walking. I skip checking in with my hiking buddies on those days, but not because I want to hide from them. It's just that I'm already a little downtrodden from having to report to my healthy-eating group: "Unwrapped seven slices of American cheese for lunch."

So I play a shell game of approval. Today my writing group won't be proud of me, but my healthy-living group will. Tomorrow I will admit to eating a bowl of my kids' cereal for breakfast but I will also gloat over having pushed the bowl aside when I finished and stayed in that seat, building and demolishing and rebuilding paragraphs for three hours.

You can't have everything.

Speaking of my kids, I am not in any accountability groups for parenting. Children hold you accountable on their own. They keep a tally, and they remind you. *Hey Mom, this is the third day we've had sandwiches for dinner. Hey Mom, we were late for carpool yesterday and the day before.* And this one, always leveled half accusingly, half compassionately: *Hey Mom, your eyes are red. Did you cry?* There's no dodging these little accountability officers. They report for duty—and report on my duties—every day.

As if kids and accountability groups weren't oversight enough, there's always Facebook and Instagram to help you feel the pressure to measure up. People say social media is making us miserable, and I don't always agree—I think there's a lot of joy and connection to be had online—but there is a downside, too. Everything online is quantified, tallied up in hearts and upturned thumbs. If a woman posts a picture of the sparkling sunrise over her morning yoga session, she's publicly delivering on her commitment to meditative stretching. When a pair of doting dads post a photo of their twins on their shoulders at the farmers' market, they're proving they've achieved optimum levels of family fun. Meanwhile, over at my house, the kids sat on the sofa with headphones on for over an hour this afternoon, because I was on the phone trying to finish an interview and I needed quiet. I will not post that. I don't want it to count.

Sometimes I feel ill-equipped to do all this accounting. (I did not take any accounting in college. Of course, in college I didn't need any help staying accountable. I had so few things to be accountable for. Show up to class, do your work, that's it.) There are days, even weeks, that I don't check in with my groups. I pull back when I feel the tail is wagging the dog, that I'm putting more energy into my anxiety over reporting what I've done than I would have put into simply doing it.

Ultimately, accountability is optional. I could leave my groups and cut myself loose from the commitment to show proof of how I use my time, but I'm self-aware enough to realize I need that sense of obligation. Knowing someone's going to ask whether I met my goals has often made me get up and do what I might otherwise have blown off, and I have better health, more pages written, and—yes—greater happiness to show for it. The encouragement helps, too. When I lost my writing time that morning in the park and started freaking out that I'd have to waste additional hours at the DMV replacing my license, my friends commiserated. They, too, have more to do than time to do it all. They urged me not to worry, it would turn up. (It did. A park ranger found my license and called the next day. I didn't lose that much time after all.)

But that's the main reason I'll always have some sort of accountability mechanism: time. I feel too keenly the need to use my minutes wisely. They will turn to seconds soon enough, and those go by too fast to count.

# Blind-Spot Detection

**The** boy who was three when we left for Ireland is now approaching sixteen.

A dozen years ago, I feared what I thought parents of three-year-olds should fear: Should he be learning another language? Am I feeding him enough protein? Is it the right protein? What if he falls in the driveway and cracks his head? What if I forget to teach him something important about how to make friends?

As fear so often does, it refused to look itself in the eyes, instead drawing my attention to problems I could solve with things I could buy—namely, the perfect double-stroller. In Dublin, we'd have no car, and our ability to go anywhere would depend on taking both children on lengthy walks to the train station. My baby daughter would need a stroller, and, though he was really too big for one, my son might sometimes need a break from walking, too. I scrolled through page after page of online reviews before settling on an ideal model. Its extra big-kid seat affixed with a secure click to its metal arms. It offered ample foot room for both passengers, a smooth ride thanks to bicycle-style wheels, and a narrow body, perfect for maneuvering down crowded city streets and onto trains. Press a lever with your foot, and the whole thing collapsed into a neatly folded rectangle. It was sturdy, efficient, sleek—and safe.

*Safe* is everything. I bought it.

Now my son is taller than me, and I fear different things. Is he happy and does he know what to do when he's not? Will he suffer or cause some terrible pain because he thoughtlessly takes one of the many stupid risks teenagers take? Or what if he takes the risk all Americans take—simply going to school or the movies, walking around in public—and he gets shot? I can't mitigate all those risks. So I obsess over cars instead.

Before my son even had his learner's permit, I was comparing the safety features of our two decade-old family automobiles, imagining which set of airbags and antilock brake system could best get him from home to school and wherever else he needs to go. Which one would handle wet roads better? Which provided optimal visibility at night?

Sometimes I think it would be ridiculous to buy a new car for a teenager. Then again, I've seen the ads: "I'm sorry. I'm okay. I'm fine," the tearful boy in the commercial says, his bumper crumpled but his body not even bruised, the impact of the crash absorbed completely by steel. New cars these days are made with features like "blind-spot detection sensors." Blind-spot detection? If only we all had it.

No wonder there's such a market for diaper bags with a dozen compartments and gizmos. They're talismans against harm for new parents just wrapping their minds around the idea that the child who has existed in their dreams for months or years will now exist in the outside world, where anything and anyone might touch him. He might at any moment need a bottle or a sweater or a developmentally appropriate toy. (He might need a stroller that deflects rain, wind, and his mother's nervousness about caring for him abroad, so far from family and friends.)

I've made so much fun of other parents when I've seen children outfitted in ridiculously high-end gear. No kid needs $20 socks. No sock delivers $20 worth of amazing.

But I know how some of those kids end up in those socks. When it comes time to send our little ones to the bus stop, we want to believe that by wrapping them in quilted goose-down jackets, packing their lunch in a temperature-controlled tote, and buttressing their growing spines with ergonomically designed backpack straps, we're as good as holding them in our arms wherever they go. We don't really believe these things will act as force fields . . . but what if?

This is how those of us with the best intentions—those who surely know better—end up overprotecting and over-indulging our children. We're not being idiots. Or we are, but only because we are human, and humans are animals, and animals instinctively protect their young. We humans just happen to have a lot of false protection available to us. We're all on a slippery slope from rational to insane, and the companies who make this stuff know it.

The frantic parental need to do every little thing right starts even before a baby is born. Have you signed up for the right prenatal classes? Washed the baby clothes in the right hypoallergenic detergent? Did you buy the right pacifier? May the Lord have mercy on your soul if you let your baby suck on a rubber nipple that causes him orthodontic misfortune later in life. WHAT WERE YOU THINKING.

If you believe there's one right answer to every child-rearing question—and I may not so much anymore, but I sure did for at least the first decade of parenting—then you're prone to extrapolating every choice you make. What if Junior doesn't get into the "best" baby music class, the one where they put all the maracas and ukuleles and xylophones out on the floor and let the tots gravitate to the instrument that calls to them? Then what? He'll never learn to play music, which means he won't develop language and spatial skills, which means he'll surely fail both English and math and never get into college. His hand-eye coordination will stall out, and he'll be unable to hold a fork. All the other kids will be conducting orchestras and building robots with their amazing fine and gross motor skills, but Junior? No, Junior will eat with his hands, miss his own mouth, and stumble through the world in Velcro shoes with peanut butter on his face. All because he didn't get on the waiting list for that music class fast enough.

We want the best for our children, even if we don't agree on what "the best" is or how to help them get it. For my mom, that meant drilling me on words so I could win a spelling bee. For me, it means studying the crash statistics of midsize vehicles. Most parents want a good future for their kids, but the details of *what* and *how* along the way aren't nearly as important as we think they are. Montessori or regular kindergarten? Cereal or hot breakfast? Summer camp or summer job? Some of it doesn't matter very much. Almost none of it matters a lot.

That's hard to see in the moment, though. I can look back now and think, *I know better than to think what brand of bib they wore made a difference.* But you couldn't have told me that then.

My son has been asking about colleges lately, and we've done some googling, inadvertently planting algorithmic seeds for the ads that now sprout in my browser. When I turned on my laptop the other day, a promotion popped up in my sidebar for "college student insurance." I read the ad—"We offer replacement cost coverage, including accidental damage, theft, fire, and natural disaster . . ."—and just about spat my coffee across the kitchen. *Replacement cost?* How do you replace a college student? Then I saw the next line, which read, ". . . for your personal electronics and other belongings." Ah.

Maybe when I fixate on strollers and cars, I'm thinking of them like insurance, an investment in my children's future. But I think it's more and crazier than that. Insurance means you get a payout if something—or someone—comes to harm, and I don't want my children to come to harm at all. I believe in resilience and learning from our pain, yes, but at the same time, counterintuitively and deep, deep down, I wonder if maybe, just this once, these kids could grow into adults unscathed, their bodies uninjured, my heart unbroken. I know it's impossible. I think about it anyway.

I don't know yet what we'll do about the car, if there is to be a car at all. The sensible side of my brain reminds me that the best way to ensure my son stays safe on the roads is to give him plenty of practice and patience. But in another part of my brain—the part that talked me into the fleece seat covers for the stroller—I wonder if there might be some essential new invention on the market. I wonder if I can trade away something so small as money in exchange for something so big as his life.

# The Joy of Quitting

I love to make people laugh.

And I love approval.

So to get the approval of being selected as an official laugh-maker by a magazine that presides over grocery store checkout lanes and pedicure chairs across the country felt like a big deal. A funny writer-friend of mine brought me on board at *Us Weekly* and explained how it works: The editors send us, the writers, a file of celebrity photos every Tuesday. On Wednesday, we each email back a list of jokes to go with each photo. The next week, a few captions for each image are chosen to run in the magazine's Fashion Police spread.

Analyzing fashion is great fun. Take gladiator sandals, for instance. They make your calves looked like pork tenderloin trussed with twine, so how did they get to be so popular? What message is a woman conveying when she wears them? *I love the feel of air on my toes and also want people to know I'm tough enough to stab a lion or errant Roman with a sword in front of a roaring crowd?* I guess.

I figured the *Us Weekly* job would be right up my alley.

———

I didn't exactly knock it out of the park at the start. To me, a deadpan, literal description of a garment is funny, but apparently that's not the style *Us Weekly* is looking to serve up to its consumers.

"Rihanna emerges from limousine, nipples mashed to two-dimensional discs by translucent bandeau compression-top." They didn't run that.

"Hair whipped into anti-gravitational balloon, Adele orders tea from behind fruit-platter-size sunglasses." Not that one either.

Knowing that we wouldn't be penalized for jokes that didn't make the cut, sometimes I sent in rambling captions like this one, on a starlet in a python-and-lace tube dress: "She looks like a very fancy snake going to a wedding where all the other snakes are like, 'Daaaaamn, girl, dontchoo know better than to upstage the snake-bride?' but she's like 'Bitch, please, I do what I want.'"

They did not run that.

I tried studying the jokes that did make the cut each week. I knew some of the other writers. They were wildly talented, but the captions running under their names weren't as funny as their other writing. It seemed the magazine was deliberately choosing the most bland, punny lines. So I tried toning down the weird, softening my humor a bit.

A shredded cape: "The fringed poncho. Froncho, if you will."

A long blazer over apparently no pants at all: "Suit yourself. Or, you know, half-suit yourself. Whatever."

A demure skirt suit with black leather hand wear: "It's all fun and crumpets until someone puts on OJ gloves."

Tiny red hot pants: "Ruby slippers take you home; ruby knickers take you everywhere."

A floral gown: "My grandmother had those curtains." That's not even a joke. It's just a statement. It ran.

Eventually, I got the hang of it and got at least a few "jokes" in every issue. I wanted them to come with a disclaimer: *I can be better than this.* But I was on a roll.

I think the only caption they ever ran that I felt really proud of was for Jane Fonda, who in her late seventies had no qualms about showing up on a red carpet in a skintight sequined green bodysuit. "The Green Lantern's mom is looking hot," I quipped. She did look hot. And she looked like the Green Lantern's mom.


I didn't like the jokes I was making to gain acceptance, but there was something else that bothered me even more. The role I put myself in to do this job made me uncomfortable. There's a difference between poking fun at professional ads or photos from a fashion runway and taking aim at what real people are wearing. No matter how funny or not-funny my captions were, this job, at its core, was poking fun at people.

Sure, some of our subjects were standing on red carpets, posing for cameras, inviting the public gaze. You could say they were asking for it. But how many of them were doing it because they really loved dressing up and posing for public consumption? How many were doing it because it was a necessary part of the job—promoting a movie or an album or receiving an award—and they couldn't let people down by saying no, or they were afraid they'd lose out on much-needed publicity for a project if they abstained? How many were dressed by a crazy stylist who said, "Trust me, this yellow vinyl bustier is a *great* idea," as a manager stood by and said, "It's fabulous, so fabulous."

And that's not even including the people who weren't on red carpets at all—whose pictures were snapped as they walked, heads down, through airports and in and out of gyms and coffee shops, going about their lives at the end of a paparazzo's long-range lens.

I wanted to look away, to give them a little space.

You could say, well, they're so famous, they shouldn't complain. You see that line of reasoning all the time: "You're the one who decided to go into show business." *You asked for it*, people imply. *It comes with the package.*

No, they didn't ask for that. Not all of them. Some of them just wanted to act—or to sing or to write—not to have a guy with a camera popping out from behind trash cans as they walk down the street. I thought about all the articles and tweets I'd read by celebrities begging the paparazzi to respect their family's privacy, all the interviews in which they described the relentless way the photogs dogged them, pouncing as soon as they exited a hotel or restaurant, following too closely in traffic, trotting along five steps behind on the sidewalk.

That's probably the first and last way in which I relate to movie stars, but I do relate. It's fair to want some parts of an experience but not all. It's fair to realize that while you did indeed mean to take every step that led you to where you are, now that you're there you realize you don't love everything about it. It's fair to say, *Stop. Not all of this is okay.*


So I had mixed feelings about this Fashion Police thing.

But I'm not a quitter. Anyone can give up on something; the trick is staying the course when things get hard, right? Rising to the challenge. Pushing through. When it feels like something can't be done, a real achiever finds a way. A real achiever doesn't squander an opportunity.

Or does she?


I blew an interview on purpose once.

It was eleventh grade, and I'd been contacted by the Governor's Honors Program—a summer camp of sorts where kids from all over the state lived on a college campus and took classes in leadership and team-building and the performing arts and calculus and all sorts of other advanced subjects. It's not something you apply for; one day you just get a letter that says, "You've been selected to interview," and you're supposed to show up and talk to somebody who will determine whether you'll be one of the lucky ones.

Except it didn't sound so lucky to me. It sounded boring. Four weeks of forced socialization with people I didn't know? School in the summer? Oh, hell no.

Summer might normally be a perfectionist kid's nightmare, what with all that time off from studying and getting grades. But summer, to me, was sacred. Sanctioned by school itself as a break from the classroom, summer existed purely by nature of the school year that surrounded it on both sides. Like the negative white space created by not painting on part of a canvas, the weeks from June through August were meant to stay blank. One could still fill them with accomplishments like reading fifty books or swimming two hundred laps or eating a Popsicle every single day for a seventy-day streak. But one should not be in school during the summer. I may have been a nerd, but I was a real human kid, too.

But what to do? I'd been *chosen*. I did like being chosen.

My gut churned as my mother drove me to the interview office.


The first several questions passed easily. What's your favorite subject? (English.) What do you do for fun? (Read.) What do you like about leadership? (Leading. And being right. And getting shit done.) Then we got to this one:

"What would you do this summer if you weren't selected for this program?"

Huh.

That's when I took a sharp turn. I did what I had never done before and wouldn't do again for a long time.

With no one watching—it was just the interviewer and me in the room—I decided that while I liked being chosen, I didn't like what I had been chosen for. As Cheap Trick said,

*I want you to want me*, but I didn't want all that came with this "honor."

So I answered: "I'd be pretty happy, actually."


I got in the car. Buckled my seat belt, eyes on the dash.

"How'd it go?" my mom asked.

"Fine, I guess."

I felt like I'd just committed murder.

My heart still races when I think of it.


One Tuesday several months into my tenure on the Fashion Police force, we received in our weekly packets a photo of the singer Kelly Clarkson wearing a T-shirt tucked into a full skirt made of fabric printed with records all over it. A music skirt! It was adorable. Also? Props for knowing how to tuck a top into a skirt, Kelly. People act like that's a skill women are born with, but I'm here to tell you, it's not. Every time I try it, the skirt ends up hiked up in the back and down in the front with my shirt blousing out around my belly like I'm Eloise.

I couldn't make fun of her or her outfit. I wanted to send in, "This is how to set a record for looking marvelous, fuckers."

I knew I couldn't send that in, so I started making a list of music puns instead, rolling my eyes at every stupid phrase I typed.

I felt like a faker.

It goes against my nature to leave a task incomplete. I've only recently been able to let myself give up on a book I don't like without reaching the last page, and to do so I had to convince myself that because part of my job is reading and evaluating books, I technically *am* completing the task by deciding which books are worth reading to the end. I've set my phone to chime and go dark at 10:20 p.m., because I know I have a habit of checking Twitter before I go to bed. It's impossible to reach the end of the internet, and without a reminder to put my phone away, I'm in danger of scroll-scroll-scrolling infinitely, scanning screen after screen of tweets as if there's a last tweet coming, a window that will pop up and say, "All done. You finished the internet. Good night."

But maybe the trick isn't sticking everything out. The trick is quitting the right thing at the right time. The trick is understanding that saying "No, thank you" to something you're expected to accept isn't failure. It's a whole other level of success.

It takes courage to quit something, but often you get that courage back with dividends. The novelist Katie Coyle once tweeted: "Last week I killed a book I've been writing for three and a half years and now I feel drunk with power." The older I get, the more I find Katie's right. A good quit feels powerful. Deciding what you won't have in your life is as important as deciding what you will have. Trying out something you expect to love, realizing you don't really love it, and giving it back, that takes guts.

It takes letting go of the idea that living right means racking up every honor you can get. It means understanding that success isn't about nailing every role; it's about choosing the roles you'll play and how well you want to play them. It's about refusing to see yourself as the passive recipient of a life someone else awards you.

The Fashion Police accepted my resignation with grace and good wishes.

# I'm Sorry, Mindy Kaling

**I'm** at an age where I know myself pretty well. There are things I do—I rise early; I floss; I ask for the dessert menu, then give it back, then wish I hadn't, then stare jealously at the cake on everyone else's plate. And there are things I do not do—I do not wear scented deodorant; I do not eat celery; I do not drink lukewarm cocktails. Not a lot of surprises here.

One thing I've known about myself for a long time is this: I do not bother celebrities. I think people deserve to have privacy, even in public, so I make a point of ignoring famous people when I see them. When I found myself in the cereal aisle of Publix with Elton John (at least I think it was Elton John), I looked down at my box of Honey Bunches of Oats, humming "Tiny Dancer" inside my head until he passed. When I bumped into Anthony Hopkins on a sidewalk in Italy (it was definitely Anthony Hopkins; I'd accidentally wandered into the periphery of a movie set), I kept walking, mostly out of deference and a little bit because I'm still scared of Hannibal Lecter.

And I know—I just *know*—that when I do this, when I respect the personal space of a famous person, they recognize it and feel grateful. I believe it forms a connection between us that is much more meaningful than the few seconds of contact they might have with some fame-whore holding out an iPhone. And I'll be honest with you, I'm a little smug about it. When I see someone walk up to Dave Grohl in the produce section at Whole Foods and start freaking out about their lifelong love of the Foo Fighters, I think, *amateur.* I've built this scenario up in my head where I'm the silent, helpful wing-woman of every celebrity I see.

I've even imagined how I would treat my favorite celebrities if I ever did run into them. Like, let's say I'm sitting at a bar, and Oprah walks up to order a drink. Probably a smoothie made of golden beets and angel wings or something.

*What could happen* is that I walk over to Oprah and yell, *OPRAH!* and make crazy eyes and put my arms out for a hug.

*What really would happen* is that I see Oprah. Oprah sees that I see Oprah; but Oprah also sees that I am acting like she is not Oprah, although she knows that I know that she's Oprah. As excitement ripples through the crowd and bar patrons begin pressing closer around her, going, "Hey, Oprah, it's you, Oprah!" we exchange a glance. And in that instant, a silent conversation takes place:

With her eyes, Oprah would say: *Everywhere I go, it's like this.*
And my eyes would say: *I know. Sorry.*

OPRAH: *Thank you. You're obviously different from the rest. We should be friends.*
ME: *We SHOULD be friends. But I'm not going to come over there and give you my phone number,*

> *because you've already got people pushing paper in your face.*
>
> OPRAH: *That's okay. By virtue of the connection we are making right now, your email address will spell itself in my organic alphabet soup when I have lunch tomorrow, and I will always know how to contact you.*
>
> ME: *I'm glad we had this moment.*
>
> OPRAH: *Me too. Thank you for respecting me.*
>
> ME: *Be well, Oprah. Be well.*

(I've thought about it a lot.)

I was in New York for a publishing conference. That evening, a crowd of book people—writers, editors, agents—had arranged themselves among the hanging ferns and tastefully threadbare rugs of the Bowery Hotel terrace at sunset to toast the actress Mindy Kaling's new memoir. I'd been up since five, having spent the day going from the Javits Convention Center out to Brooklyn bookshops and back again signing copies of my own book, *Penguins with People Problems*, a slim volume of illustrated humor. Still tucked into my pocket was the flat cartoon penguin character I'd been using as a prop. I smoothed its laminated wings with my thumb as I chatted with a friend and silently admired Arianna Huffington's shoes.

An hour into the party, Kaling still had not shown, and expectant partygoers were checking their watches and glancing around. I scoffed. Everyone was anxiously fretting over whether they'd get a moment with her, a photo, some souvenir of experience. Not me. Heck, I might even leave.

Then the buzz started: "Mindy's downstairs! She's almost here! Mindy! Mindy! Mindy!" Guests jostled for position along the exposed brick wall by the door.

The tension rose and the over-the-shoulder glances grew more anxious. The guest of honor appeared in the doorway; then the tide of humanity lifted her and she was buoyed along the crowd. Within seconds, she landed right in front of me. I stood face-to-face with Mindy Kaling, and this is what I said:

"OH MY GOD, HI MINDY KALING. I LOVE YOUR BOOKS AND YOUR SHOW, MINDY KALING."

I informed her of her own name. Twice.

Perhaps it was the sudden real-life presence, just inches from my face, of this entertainer I'd long admired that caused my behavioral short circuit. Perhaps I was just tired, and the starstruck atmosphere had infected my weakened system like a virus. Or maybe I sensed in a split second that this was our chance to meet and be friends, but my mouth couldn't catch up with my brain's message to say a simple hello and smile. All I know is what happened next:

I held out the penguin-on-a-stick that was in my hand, offering it to her as if it were a glass of wine.

When I recall that moment, I don't remember making a decision. I didn't think, *You know what I should do right now? I should take this cartoon animal and place it into the hands of the person standing before me whom I don't know, with no explanation.* I just did it.

"Do you want . . . a picture?" she asked. I nodded.

"Maybe you should hold that," she said, pointing at the penguin. I pulled it back. Suddenly, I was doing everything *I do not do*. I flapped my hair behind my ears again and again. I tried to remember what my younger colleagues had taught me about taking selfies. Was it stick the chin out or suck the chin in?

My friend took the photo. Mindy Kaling walked away. I stood there holding a cardboard bird, wondering what had just happened.

I've thought about that evening again and again, reliving my embarrassment in waves, and sending my apology out into the universe in hopes it would reach her: I was an idiot, and I'm sorry, Mindy Kaling.

But there's something else about that moment that has occurred to me recently. I've decided that if I ever see Mindy Kaling again, I'll make only the most minimal eye contact, and it will go something like this:

Mindy Kaling's eyes: *Oh no, not you again.*

My eyes: *Wait. Remember how I turned into a weirdo fangirl at that party? I didn't even know that version of me existed until then. And if that person was somewhere inside me, just waiting for her moment to emerge, who else might be in there? Imagine.*

Before I turn away as if I don't even see her, I'll nod a little thank-you, and Mindy will understand.

# Try It Again, More Like You

**As** soon as the cameras start rolling, I freeze.

I'm supposed to introduce the guest and say my opening lines, "Welcome to *A Word on Words*. I'm Mary Laura Philpott, and today we're talking to . . ." but suddenly my ability to modulate my own volume and pronounce vocabulary in the language I've been speaking all my life has left me. I'm yelling: WELCOME! TO! AWORDONWORDS! I'm MARY-LAURAPHILPOTT! AND TODAYWERETALKIN! I sound like the robo-voice of a 1990s answering machine on high speed—Please! Leave! Amessage! Afterthetone!

Matt laughs. He's operating one of the cameras, and because this is public television and everyone has at least two roles at the same time, he's also our editor, the one who will later take all the rough interview footage and weave it together into a finished show. I know why he's laughing. This happens every time.

He leans out from around the camera.

"Try it again, more like you," he says.

I take a deep breath and start over.

-----

The problem comes when I think about the role I'm playing instead of the thing I'm doing. I can discuss nitty-gritty life-and-literature stuff with anyone, anywhere, all day long. But when I become aware of the camera and of my job as an interviewer, the halting emphasis on random syllables starts up again: "What's the se-CRET to a great co-MED-ic no-VEL? Today we'll TALKTOTHEAUTHOR! ANDFINDOUT!"

We came to an agreement, Matt and I. He understood that it would take me a few rounds of filming the intro before I'd loosen up enough to record a keeper. And I trusted that he'd tell me when I screwed up, so I could fix it. The whole team knew I was inexperienced. They'd known ever since the first time I looked into the camera and spoke my name during the screen test, sitting on my hands to keep from scratching the rash on my face.

"I'm—wait, where do I look?"

"Into the camera."

It felt strange and impersonal to address the rectangular lens and not the person whose outline I could just make out beyond it. I knew the crew was there in the shadows, but I couldn't make out their faces. The cavernous Nashville Public Television studio—two stories high and packed along each wall with discarded set pieces—was completely dark, except for the spot where I sat in a tall director's chair, lit by a beam coming from somewhere behind the camera. The NPT producers had invited me to come do a screen test to be considered as a host of *A Word on Words*, an author interview show. I'd never done on-camera work before, but the folks who produced the show had seen some of my writing about books and thought

I might be a good candidate for a host. I love talking about books, so I said sure.

The week before the screen test, I'd treated myself to a facial, which I knew damn well was a bad idea. I've had maybe four facials in my life. It always takes me a while to forget my sensitive skin's unforgiving policy on unfamiliar emollients; but then I get sucked into a tranquil-looking advertisement and think, *Yes, I* would *become a relaxed person if I let a stranger massage mystery oils into my face for an hour.* My skin started boiling with bumps a few hours after I left the day spa. By the next day, it looked like I'd tried to cure a severe case of acne by rubbing my cheeks with poison ivy. I did not look or feel like myself when I screen-tested; I felt like a raw hamburger patty crawling with ants, being filmed for a nature documentary. That they took a chance and let me come back and shoot a pilot episode is a miracle.

If you take one thing from this story, let it be that you should never get a facial before recording a television show.

That's not the only lesson I got from my first television job. In addition, I learned: You must turn off your clip-on microphone before going to the bathroom. It takes professional drag queen levels of makeup not to look washed out under the lights. If you sit comfortably, you'll look on-screen as if you're slumped over in your chair like a corpse; you must hold the electrified posture of a startled ballerina if you want to look like you're sitting up straight.

Also, when you interview someone, you have to sit very

close to them in order to be in the same frame. It looks normal on TV, but in real life it feels like you're invading each other's personal space.

At the end of shooting an interview, there's always an odd part of the process where the camera guys get right up next to us and shoot footage of our hands and faces. Each person is supposed to smile and nod as if listening to the other talk, but we can't actually speak. We're also supposed to make conversational hand gestures—clasping and unclasping, pointing, turning our palms up in a "so, you see . . ." kind of way. Then, when they're editing the interview, they've got reaction shots of our hands and faces they can splice in wherever they need them. But this means that for about three minutes, we're looking at each other and nodding, while folding and unfolding our hands, without saying a word. Again, looks great on TV, feels super-weird in real life.

I'll never forget the time we had the Pulitzer Prize–winning novelist Elizabeth Strout on the show. I had decided that I'd make the hands-and-faces bit at the end more fun by putting on some music to fill the silence. Her latest book at the time was called *Anything Is Possible*, so I picked out a song by Ben Folds called "Capable of Anything." Similar themes.

What I didn't foresee was that by playing music I was making the moment not less uncomfortable, but much more so. It's a surprisingly intimate experience to look into someone's eyes at close range without speaking for the length of a song, not to mention a song about discovering the hitherto unknown depths of one's soul. I realized almost immediately that I'd made the whole thing weirder, but once we were rolling, we couldn't stop.

So there we sat, so near to each other that our knees touched, gazing and nodding and hand-waving like mimes to a Ben Folds serenade. She was such a good sport—when the cameras stopped, she said, "Well, we just had a moment!"—but I felt like such a creeper for subjecting her to those three minutes.

Sometimes fighting the awkwardness just makes everything more awkward. Now I know.


Making art—painting, singing, what have you—is never as easy as the final product makes it look. Take drawing, for instance. You might look at a picture of a dog and think, *I'm going to draw a dog, too!* And then as you attempt to draw a dog, you realize that this dog you've pictured in your mind isn't quite coming across on paper. You might think, *I want this shaggy dog to look friendly and whimsical.* But when you put your pen to paper, you can't figure out how to move your hand to make the ink convey friendly and whimsical. You have to concentrate on so many technical things: the right pressure to apply to make the fur look furry, the properly curved lines of the dog's mouth, the proportion of legs to head to torso to tail. It doesn't feel whimsical at all as you throw away your nineteenth try and start your twentieth drawing of that dog. These aren't things the viewer thinks about, but they're the things you have to do as the creator. You work, work, work on making something that will not feel at all like work in its consumption.

I knew this already about writing, but I had not yet learned it about television. In writing, you can go off and do the hard, technical work-stuff in sweatpants while hunched over a laptop for hours that turn into years, then step back, put on a clean dress, and hold the final, polished, packaged book out to readers. Ta-da!

When filming, you have to be the polished, packaged thing on camera AND you have to do the technical work of looking into the correct lens AND you have to talk and have a personality and listen and think and keep the conversation moving.

Writing has more phases; filming is all at once. But that's why it's nice to be allowed several takes.

Once to look into the right camera.

Twice to get the words right.

Three times to slow down and breathe normally.

Four times to forget all that and just talk.

You have to blink back the spell the camera casts on you, remember that you're just a person sitting in a chair across from another person, having a chat. Do your preparation before, yes, but when the moment comes, let go. Don't think about all the things that are happening at the same time. Surrender to the moment, be open to surprise, and follow where the conversation goes. This is what makes for a good show.

I used to think that if only I could make everything perfect, then I could relax and have fun. If I could just eliminate all mistakes, my life would settle into place—*click!*—and my mind would rest. If I'm being truthful, I have to acknowledge that on some unchangeable, deep-down level, there's still a part of me that thinks that. I'm still a first grader at a spelling bee, thinking that what matters more than anything is that I get every single word right.

But by now, I've built up a crowd of selves who can set that little girl at ease. *It's okay*, they tell her. *Mistakes will happen—they have happened—and it's not the end of the world.* They get her to loosen up a little. They help her see that doing things wrong is part of doing life right. They show her that joy is bigger than fear. It can even be funny when things go haywire.

So scratch the thing about never getting a facial before recording a television show. I mean, don't get the pre-TV facial—it's a bad idea. But if you're going to take just one thing from this story, let it be something much more important:

You can always start over.

Sometimes my guests, especially the debut authors who haven't done much press yet, stumble over their words or forget someone's name or blurt out a thought they didn't really mean to share. A look of panic always crosses their face when that happens, but there's no need to worry, I tell them. I put my hand on theirs and say, *It's fine. We have plenty of time. Try it again, more like you.*

# Acknowledgments

*Thank you* —

To Kristyn Keene, for whom the word *agent* is insufficient, and to Trish Todd and the team at Simon & Schuster, for believing in and cheering for this book before it even was a book. Special thanks also to Cat Shook at ICM and to these folks at Simon & Schuster: the amazing Jessica Roth and Wendy Sheanin, plus the brilliant Kaitlin Olson, Meredith Vilarello, Kelsey Manning, Cherlynne Li, Tara Parsons, Susan Moldow, Polly Watson, and the team at Atria. And a million high fives to Beth Parker, of course.

To friends and colleagues in Nashville, Atlanta, New York, and all over the country—more of you than I could mention here without using up a whole tree's worth of pages—for giving expert advice, letting me talk your ears off, or generally showing kindness and patience while I worked on this project. (If you think I might mean you, I do.) Extra thanks for the friendship to Brittany Roberts, Susannah Parker, and Laura Balch; to my Davidson gang; and to the Loose Women Book Club, especially Sissy Gardner.

To my writing group—Margaret Renkl, Susannah Felts,

Maria Browning, and Carrington Fox. Every other writing group wishes they were as great as you. Thanks also to the very early readers brave enough to sit through a whole draft, including Molly Schulman, Ashton Hickey, Catherine Bock, plus Emmely Duncan and Kelly Kirby-Piovarcy, who read some pretty rough drafts. And to Keltie Peay for emergency proofreading.

To Amy Williams for name-dropping me into a conversation that started another conversation that started another conversation that led to my finally sitting down and writing this thing.

To Carmen Toussaint and Rivendell Writers Colony for space and time.

To the animals who made the human world more tolerable during the writing of this book: Eleanor Roosevelt, Woodstock, Frank, Thaquine, Leonard, Sparky, Emma, Clark, Millie, Biddy, Tillie, Alice, Faye, the ever-evolving cast of shop dogs, parking-lot cats, and internet bats.

To Linda Wei, Matt Emigh, and the whole crew at Nashville Public Television for the line "try it again, more like you," which I'll be using forever.

To Roberta Zeff, Rachel Dry, KJ Dell'Antonia, Nadja Spiegelman, Amy Joyce, Towles Kintz, Nora Krug, Ron Charles, and other editors over the years for publishing my essays along the way, including some of the work that would eventually end up in this book.

To independent bookstores everywhere.

To each member of my bookstore family at Parnassus Books. Extra thanks to Karen Hayes, who provided endless support as I attempted to cram bookstore work, writing work, and parent work into the confines of twenty-four-hour days.

## ACKNOWLEDGMENTS

To Colin Meloy and the Decemberists for allowing me to borrow their lyrics about a boy band and turn them into an epigraph about womanhood and reinvention.

To my family, especially my parents, for loving me.

To WC and MG, for letting me love you.

To John, the most.

# Previously Published

Parts of the following essays, published by these outlets, appear in some form this book:

*New York Times*
   "Shopping for a Car—and a Teenager's Future"
   "My Adventures in Accountability"
   "Sing, O Muse, of the Mall of America"
   "Wishing Away the Wish List"
   "And Then the Dog Died"
   "Telling the Kids: We're Moving"

*Washington Post*
   "Teaching Girls to Save Their Own Lives"

*Los Angeles Times*
   "How Prince's Death Stirs Fans' Concerns for Their Heroes"

*Paris Review*
   "The Case for Seasonal Sentimentality"

*Proximity*
   "Lobsterman"